The Reformed Apprentice
Volume 3: A Workbook on the Doctrine of God
By C. Matthew McMahon, Ph.D., Th.D.

Copyright Information

The Reformed Apprentice Volume 3: A Workbook on the Doctrine of God
By C. Matthew McMahon

Edited by Therese B. McMahon
Copyright © 2015 by Puritan Publications and A Puritan's Mind

Published by Puritan Publications
A Ministry of A Puritan's Mind
3971 Browntown Road
Crossville, TN 38572
www.puritanpublications.com
www.apuritansmind.com
www.puritanshop.com

All rights reserved. No part of this publication may be reproduced, stored in a retrieval system or transmitted in any form by any means, electronic, mechanical, photocopy, recording or otherwise, without the prior permission of the publisher, except as provided by USA copyright law.

First Electronic Edition, 2015
First Print Edition, 2015
Manufactured in the United States of America

ISBN: 978-1-62663-126-7
eISBN: 978-1-62663-125-0

Front cover image is a photograph of "The Scholar at the Table" by Belgian painter Emile Charles Wauters, (1846-1933).

Contents

The Reformed Apprentice Volume 3: A Workbook on the Doctrine of God	1
Copyright Information	2
Contents	3
Introduction	4
The Doctrine of God	10
God's Divine Attributes	24
The Trinity	63
The Divinity of the Son	68
The Divinity of the Holy Spirit	99
The Decrees of God	117
Concluding Remarks	129
Test Yourself	132

Introduction

"In the beginning God..." (Genesis 1:1).

This volume is the third in a series of workbooks that will cover a biblical view of God housed in Reformed Theology. The first volume was dedicated to an overview of 1) being apprenticed by the best Reformed theologians and preachers of church history, and 2) covering the basic aspects of Reformed Theology. It answered the question, "What does it mean to be Reformed?" The second workbook covered the doctrine of Scripture and of Biblical interpretation (the science of hermeneutics). It helped answer, "Why is the Bible the Word of God?" and "How do I interpret the Bible?" This third workbook is going to answer, "Who is God?" and, "What is God like?" We will especially look at God in the three persons of the Trinity as Father, Son and Spirit. Interestingly, God's revealed will as it is stated in his inerrant and infallible word, is first *assumptive*.

What does it mean to *assume* something?

_____
_____
_____
_____

The first part of Genesis 1:1 what does the verse assume? Or better yet, what does the verse *not* attempt to prove right out of the gate?

_____
_____
_____
_____
_____

What is the relevance of God not beginning with proving his existence?

_____
_____
_____
_____
_____

As with each of the volumes in this Reformed series, the goal of this workbook is to love God and Jesus Christ more today than you did yesterday. These workbooks are not designed as simply exercises for you to flex your theological muscles. Those who have worked through the last two books have heard this before. But I will continue to beat this drum because any study of God's word is not simply an intellectual exercise. It is primarily to gain the real blessing of the Spirit, further conformity to the image of Jesus Christ, and a deeper fellowship with the Father. With every subsequent volume in this series, this goal will continue to be pressed and you will need to answer your goals for this workbook with biblical answers.

Take a moment to write down *your goal* for the study in the space below. Relate that goal to the purpose of this workbook – understanding that this workbook is going to deal with *knowing* God. What is *your* goal for this study?

YOUR GOAL OF VOLUME 3:

_____
_____
_____
_____
_____

Introduction

SYSTEMATIC THEOLOGY

When dealing with one of the most important subjects in human history, the doctrine of God, the Reformed Apprentice must come to terms with the inevitable – they are going to be turned into systematicians. What is that? A systematicican is someone who systematically deals with God's word to determine what it says "comprehensively" about a specific doctrine. This is where we get *systematic theology* from.

How would you define systematic theology?

_____
_____
_____
_____
_____

I love reading *Systematic Theology* books. Obviously, some are better than others. Some are more orthodox, more detailed, more helpful, and even more anointed. None are perfect. My favorites are five in scope, *aside* from holding to the systematic nature of my confession of faith, *The 1647 Westminster Confession of Faith*. First, Calvin's *Institutes of the Christian Religion*, which is, for all intents and purposes, a systematic treatment of the theology found in the Bible. Second, Francis Turretin's three volume, *Institutes of Elenctic Theology* which is one of the hardest intellectual and theological works to wade through, but extremely rewarding. Third, William Ames' *The Marrow of Theology*, which reads like biblical stereo instructions being chock full of precise theological syllogisms and short paragraphs filled with rich thoughts packed with biblical insight and practical application. Fourth, Charles Hodge's *Systematic Theology* which houses tons of quotes, is very thorough, has lots of Latin, Hebrew and Greek and also runs *three* volumes. Then finally, it would be a toss-up between Berkof's *Systematic Theology* and possibly Shedd's *Reformed Dogmatics*. There are others that are helpful, but these are my favorites. The problem with all of them is that they are extremely long, intellectually heavy, and were not written for the average reader. Berkhof's work is only 800 pages or so, but it leaves out a few key doctrines in his systematic treatment (like the doctrine of

Scripture!) which makes it inadequate. There are shorter, more tolerable works like Nicholas Byfield's, "The Pattern of Wholesome Words," which covers the major points of theology, or even those that are far more technical like John Arrowsmith's "Armelia Catechetica," which covers specific points in greater detail. What does the new student of the Bible do (or someone who wants a refresher) when they come to the important subject of reading a reformed systematic theology work? Are you simply bound to one of these *giant* works? Or maybe you are a little further along in the faith and you need something a bit more thought provoking than some of the summary works. There are *not* many choices published today for this purpose. And when the new student or laymen obtains a book that is technically difficult, and really long, they tend to give up quickly on reading it through. I've personally put together an introductory work on systematic theology called, "Systematic Theology Made Easy." It is a condensed, simplistic version of a systematic theology work that covers all the major doctrines of the bible. It is set in a format that is, 1) easy to understand, and, 2) not presented in the voluminous technical jargon that systematic theology professors often revel in. However, it is not a workbook. It is rather, something to personally study.

In dealing with Systematic Theology there are usually two matters that are dealt with before formally getting into doctrine. One is defining theology. The second is where we find theology, which is the doctrine of Scripture. Since volume 2 of this workbook series already dealt with the doctrine of Scripture, and volume 1 already dealt with a definition of theology, you should be adequately able to answer the follow questions...right?

What is *theology*?

_____

_____

_____

_____

_____

_____

_____

Introduction

How would you explain to an unbeliever the message of Scripture?

How would you explain that Scripture is in fact *God*'s word?

Is Scripture inerrant? Why?

Is Scripture infallible? Why?

Think of Scripture as Christ's love letter to *you*. How does this elevate your thoughts of the Bible as something special to *you*?

_____
_____
_____
_____
_____

The Doctrine of God

"I am the LORD, and there is none else." (Isaiah 45:6).

Before we study the most sublime doctrine in the history of the universe, I want you to consider the following two quotes. These quotes help us with thinking rightly about who God is.

> "There is but one only living and true God, who is infinite in being and perfection, a most pure spirit, invisible, without body, parts, or passions, immutable, immense, eternal, incomprehensible, almighty, most wise, most holy, most free, most absolute, working all things according to the counsel of his own immutable and most righteous will, for his own glory; most loving, gracious, merciful, long-suffering, abundant in goodness and truth, forgiving iniquity, transgression, and sin; the rewarder of them that diligently seek him; and withal most just and terrible in his judgments; hating all sin, and who will by no means clear the guilty," (*1647 Westminster Confession of Faith* 2:1).

From the first quote above, list in the space provided the words that you are unable to *instantly* define or understand.

_____
_____
_____
_____

> "God hath all life, glory, goodness, blessedness, in and of himself; and is alone in and unto himself all-sufficient, not standing in need of any creatures which he hath made, nor deriving any glory from them, but only manifesting his own glory in, by, unto, and upon them: he is the alone fountain of all being, of whom, through whom, and to whom are all things; and hath most sovereign dominion over them, to do by them, for them, or upon them whatsoever himself pleaseth. In his sight all things are open and manifest; his knowledge is infinite, infallible, and independent upon the creature; so as nothing is to him contingent or uncertain. He is most holy in all his counsels, in all his works, and in all his commands. To him is due from angels and men, and every other creature, whatsoever worship, service, or obedience, he is pleased to require of them, (1647 *Westminster Confession of Faith* 2:2).

From the second quote above, list in the space provided the concepts *or* words that you are unable to *instantly* define or understand.

_____
_____
_____
_____
_____

Knowledge of God

All men have *some* knowledge that God exists. This knowledge of God is what we call *innate knowledge.* This means knowledge is part of, or built into, our constitution, as sentient, rational, and moral beings. The word *innate* simply indicates the source of the knowledge. It is inside us already. That source is our nature which is born with us. The mind is so built by God that it perceives certain things to be true without proof and without instruction. Such knowledge should excite us to be more interested in God. But due to the fall of man, our hearts were darkened and our minds corrupted. As a result, that knowledge is warped and out of tune with the manner in which it should be used.

> "Knowledge of God *faithfully* received suffices to inflame our minds with the love of God, and leads our lives well and happily."
> Peter Du Moulin (1568-1658)

What does Peter Du Moulin mean when he says *"faithfully received?"*

_____
_____
_____
_____
_____

Innate knowledge can be seen in the example of when we apprehend the idea of "sameness." One thing is "the same" as another thing. Here is the letter "a" and here is another letter "a". They are the same. They look the same. No one taught you "sameness." *Sameness* is an innate quality built into our constitution that recognizes that one thing looks like another. The knowledge of God is innate in this way.

How *much* knowledge do men have of God innately? They have this knowledge *generally speaking.* It is in the general sense of a Being on whom we are dependent and to whom we are responsible. It is a general knowledge of the Law of God (God's character) which is written on the heart.

The Law of God is a reflection of God's character. What does this mean?

_____
_____
_____
_____
_____

{ "So, when the people of Israel are delivered from Egypt, the Law of God follows," (*Directions for the Private Reading of the Scriptures*). Nicholas Byfield (1579-1622) }

Why is it important that the people of God, upon deliverance from Egypt and slavery, (which is a type of the Christian's deliverance from sin), received the Law of God?

_____
_____
_____
_____
_____

Every civilization that has ever existed demonstrates this Law in their writings and history no matter how off the mark they may be about the specifics of the one true "God". Such *innate* knowledge is universal. The Bible asserts that this knowledge of God *is* universal. It does this both directly and by necessary implication. The Apostle Paul says, "Because that when they *knew God* they glorified him not as God, neither were thankful," (Rom. 1:19-21). The Bible takes for granted that the knowledge of God is universal and that it is written on the heart of every man. As a result, such a knowledge and belief in God is *necessary*.

PROVING GOD

Theism is the doctrine of a personal God, the creator, preserver, and governor of the world. The design of all arguments on this subject is to show that the facts around us in the world we live in and observe, and the facts of consciousness, necessitate the assumption of the existence of such a Being. The arguments usually urged on this subject are the Ontological, the Cosmological, the Teleological, and the Moral. These are not infallible proofs, but they will serve to help the student become more attune to thinking about arguments concerning the existence of something greater than the material universe.

THE ONTOLOGICAL ARGUMENT

The ontological argument (the argument from "being") teaches: that which exists in reality is greater than that which exists only in the mind. We have an idea of an infinitely perfect Being. The actual existence is included in infinite perfection of which we could not conceive of anything greater. God is the highest truth, the highest being, the highest good, of whom all other truth and good are the manifestations. This being exists necessarily because He is the greatest and best of beings.

THE COSMOLOGICAL ARGUMENT

This argument teaches the existence of a Creator based on a sufficient cause. Every effect must have an adequate cause. The world is an effect, therefore the world must have had a cause outside of itself for its existence. This is provided that the world can be proved to be an effect, and that it is not self-caused or eternal – which is rather easy to do, based on the second law of thermodynamics which simply states that everything is degrading, not enhancing.

The world is an effect and is not self-existent or eternal. It is, in all its parts and composition, dependent and mutable. We are forced to assume the existence of an eternal and necessary Being. The argument is that if everything in the world is contingent, then this eternal and necessary Being must be a necessary *First Cause*.

THE TELEOLOGICAL ARGUMENT

This argument teaches that design supposes a designer. The world everywhere exhibits marks of design. Therefore the world owes its existence to an intelligent author. The designed world has an end that has been selected by the Author. This presupposes a choice of suitable means for its end as well as the application of those means for the accomplishment of the proposed end. This demonstrates the Author as one having intelligence, will, and power. The designer must be an external agent as something existing prior to the end product. Thus, wherever, or whenever, we see evidence of design we are convinced that it is a result of the operation of the mind of the Author. Throughout this vast universe, order reigns. In the midst of endless variety, there is unity; there is design.

This thought is constantly stated in the Bible. Paul says, "And saying, Sirs, why do ye these things? We also are men of like passions with you, and preach unto you that ye should turn from these vanities unto the living God, which made heaven, and earth, and the sea, and all things that are therein: Who in times past suffered all nations to walk in their own ways. Nevertheless he left not himself without witness, in that he did good, and gave us rain from heaven, and fruitful seasons, filling our hearts with food and gladness," (Act 14:15-17). In Romans 1:20 he said, "For the invisible things of him from the creation of the world are clearly seen, being understood by the things that are made, even his eternal power and Godhead; so that they are without excuse." God's attributes and power are clearly seen in that which is made.

THE MORAL ARGUMENT

This argument teaches morality based on an objective reality. God is what the nature of the human soul declares Him to be. Every human has in his own nature the evidence of the existence of God which forces conviction between right and wrong. Man has in himself evidence that God is an objective personal Being who is intelligent, voluntary, and moral. Man knows that God knows him, has the right to command him, and that God can punish as well as save. Man has a sense of right and wrong. He perceives or judges some things to be right, and other things to be wrong. Such judgments concern moral judgments and have an authority from which we cannot excuse ourselves. Such judgments depend on an objective reality of Lordship and Law, or a rule or standard to which we are bound to be conformed. When we judge something as "right" we are judging that according to God's Law. When we judge something to be wrong, we judge that it is not conformed to God's Law. Such Laws do not stem from us. They are set objective realities grounded in the moral nature of the Creator who requires certain actions from rational creatures. Without such an objective reality that innately dictates to us moral conscious choices, then each individual person would have the ability to determine their own morality and others could not, and would not be allowed, to be indignant at the most horrific crimes committed, or the most debased morality exhibited. A pedophile's desires would be equally valid as a rapists', as would a serial killer, as would the atrocious works of Hitler.

THE KNOWLEDGE OF THE BIBLICAL GOD

When dealing with the knowledge of God, the first question posed is "Can God be known?" The second question is "How?" And the third question is "If God can be known, how do we perceive Him correctly?"

GOD CAN BE KNOWN

The Bible teaches that God *can* be known. It teaches that eternal life *consists* in the knowledge of God and of Jesus Christ, His one and only Son. Psalm 76:1 states, "In Judah is God known: his name is great in Israel." Isaiah 11:9 states, "They shall not hurt nor destroy in all my holy mountain: for the earth shall be full of the knowledge of the LORD, as the waters cover the sea." The Apostle Peter says in 2 Peter 3:18, "They shall not hurt nor destroy in all my holy mountain: for the earth shall be full of the knowledge of the LORD, as the waters cover the sea."

This does not mean that Christians can know *all that is true* concerning God. We cannot "comprehend God" (know Him completely and fully), rather, we "apprehend" God, (understand Him in part as to what He has revealed to us about Himself).

> "*Theology*, is the science of living blessedly forever. Blessed life arises from the knowledge of God. John 17:3, "This is life eternal, that they know you to be the only very God, and whom you hast sent Christ Jesus." Isa. 53:11, "By his knowledge shall my righteous servant (*viz. Christ*) justify many." And therefore it arises likewise from the knowledge of ourselves, because we know God by looking into ourselves. Theology has two parts. The first part concerns God, the second part concerns his works," (*Golden Chain*).
>
> William Perkins (1558-1602)

What does Perkins mean when he says "Blessed life arises from the knowledge of God?"

_____
_____
_____
_____
_____

How do you know you have this "blessed life"? Use *Scripture* to fortify your answer, not personal experience.

_____
_____
_____

_____
_____
_____
_____
_____

GOD IS INCONCEIVABLE AND INCOMPREHENSIBLE

God is without limits, and thus, He who is infinite is *incapable* of having any limitation. Our minds are limited. They are not infinite. Because of this, the infinite God is inconceivable.

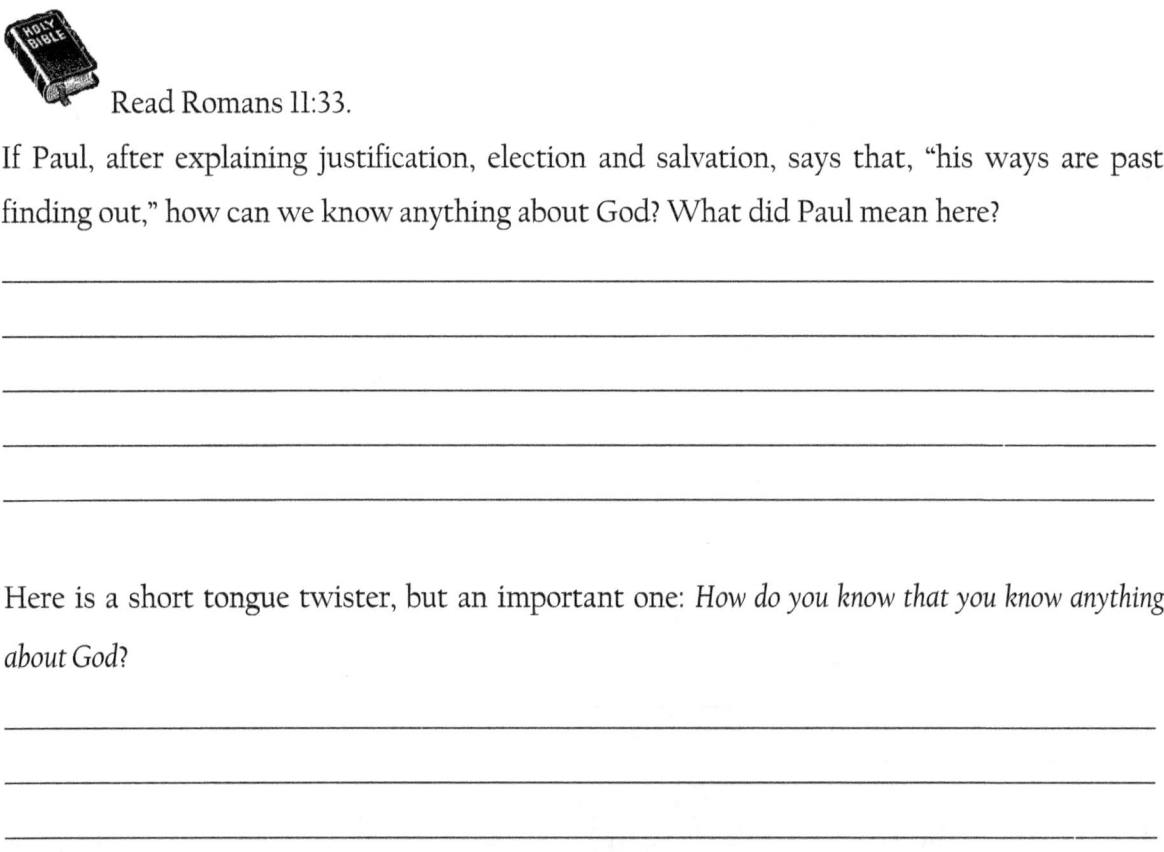 Read Romans 11:33.

If Paul, after explaining justification, election and salvation, says that, "his ways are past finding out," how can we know anything about God? What did Paul mean here?

_____
_____
_____
_____
_____

Here is a short tongue twister, but an important one: *How do you know that you know anything about God?*

_____
_____
_____
_____
_____

We cannot form a representative image of God in our minds (which is forbidden according to the second commandment). Not that we cannot believe certain teachings about God as He has revealed Himself, but that we have no point in which we can formulate an entire depiction of Him *completely*. This is part of the reason no limited image can be representative of him. It is a false image because it cannot demonstrate God adequately. In this way, God is inconceivable. He cannot be fully conceived by a finite mind.

God is also incomprehensible. He cannot be comprehended (*i.e.* we cannot have a complete and exhaustive knowledge of him). We cannot understand the Almighty God *perfectly*. In this way, our knowledge of God is partial. From Scripture we know that God knows, feels, loves, acts, *etc.* but we do not know His feelings, emotions, actions, knowledge, *etc. completely*. There is much in God which we do not know at all, and that what we do know, we know imperfectly. However, our knowledge of God as it is stated in the Bible, or innately, as far as such knowledge can go, is *true* knowledge.

If we have a partial knowledge of God, how do we know it is true? Could it be that we are missing some integral part of knowledge that would cause us to have a misconception of him? How can we be safe in what we know of God?

_____
_____
_____
_____
_____

HOW DO WE KNOW GOD?

How does our mind form its idea of God? Some answer this by way of negation. In other words we say "God is infinite", *i.e. not* finite. Paul assumed this in address to the Athenians in Acts 17:29, "Forasmuch then as we are the offspring of God, we ought not to think that the Godhead is like unto gold, or silver, or stone, graven by art and man's device." God has not communicated Himself to us in complete positives, but only in *apprehended* positives. He is holy, just, loving, *etc.* which correspond to that which we are able to understand. This type of communication is called an *anthropomorphism*. God communicates in human terms that we are able to apprehend. This was finally culminated in the writings of His Word in the Bible, and the manifestation of the Logos, or Word of God, in the person of Jesus Christ.

 Read Exodus 15:8 and Psalm 91:4.

The heretic, Brigham Young, one of the main prophets of Mormonism, says, "Some would have us believe that God is present everywhere. It is not so," (JoD 6:345). Joseph Smith, Mormonism's founder says, "The Father has a body of flesh and bones as tangible as man's…" (Doctrine and Covenants, 130:22).

Exodus 15:8 says God parted the Red Sea with a blast of his nostrils. So, God has a *nose*. It must be an awfully big nose since the Red Sea is quite large. There are Scriptures that show God has an "outstretched arm" and that he "sits" on a throne. Exodus 7:5, "And the Egyptians shall know that I am the Lord, when I *stretch out My hand* on Egypt and bring out the sons of Israel from their midst." Num. 6:24, "The Lord make *His face* shine on you, and be gracious to you." Psalm 33:6, "By the word of the Lord the heavens were made, and by the breath of His *mouth* all their host." Psalm 34:15, "The *eyes* of the Lord are toward the righteous, and His *ears* are open to their cry." Psalm 89:10, "Thou Thyself didst crush Rahab like one who is slain; Thou didst scatter Thine enemies with Thy *mighty arm*." That is why heretical sects often see God as the one with the big white beard sitting in golden lights on a big throne in some humanized form. It seems he is like a man who has bodily parts. However, at the same time, Scripture says that God has *feathers*. Now God is a chicken. Psalm 57:1, "Be gracious to me, O God, be gracious to me, for my soul takes refuge in Thee; and in the shadow of *Thy wings* I will take refuge, until destruction passes by."

In belaboring this, think about the manner in which God communicates to us. Why *does* God use human terms to communicate with us? Does God really have feathers? or a big nose?

_____
_____
_____
_____
_____

["As soon as anyone has devised an image of God, they have instituted false worship. The object of Moses is to restrain the rashness of men, lest they should travesty God's glory by their imaginations," (*Treatise on Relics*).
John Calvin (1509-1564)]

Why does Calvin link creating a mental image of God the way we think he might look, to instituting false worship?

_____
_____
_____
_____
_____

The Bible, God's divine revelation of Himself, gives man *real* knowledge. It teaches man what God is, what sin is, the law, Christ, the plan of salvation, and the state of the soul after death, *etc.* The knowledge we receive from the Bible is real in the sense that the ideas which we gain from Scripture help us to form true ideas about how God and His works really are. God and Christ, holiness and sin, heaven and hell, *really are* what the Bible declares them to be, and they are non-contradictory. They are true. Even though we only have partial knowledge of God, that knowledge is true knowledge because Scripture is clear.

DEFINITIONS OF GOD

When we say the Bible *defines* God, what we mean is that we are able to formulate the idea of God as it lies in our mind represented by the truth of His Word. The best definition is found in the *Westminster Confession* as we have already quoted, "There is but one only living and true God, who is infinite in being and perfection, a most pure spirit, invisible, without body, parts, or passions, immutable, immense, eternal, incomprehensible, almighty, most wise, most holy, most free, most absolute, working all things according to the counsel of his own immutable and most righteous will, for his own glory; most loving, gracious, merciful, long-suffering, abundant in goodness and truth, forgiving iniquity, transgression, and sin; the rewarder of them that diligently seek him; and withal most just and terrible in his judgments; hating all sin, and who will by no means clear the guilty." The Westminster Divines used the following to prove out this section of the Confession: Deut. 6:4; 1 Cor. 8:4, 6; Jer. 10:10; 1 Thess. 1:9; Job 11:7-9; 26:14; John 4:24; 1 Tim. 1:17; f. Deut. 4:15-16; John 4:24 Luke 24:39; Acts 14:11, 15; Mal. 3:6; James 1:17; 1 Kings 8:27; Jer. 23:23-24; Psa. 90:2; 1 Tim 1:17; Psa. 145:3; Gen 17:1; Rev 4:8; Rom 16:27; Isa. 6:3; Rev 4:8; Psa. 115:3; Exod. 3:14; Eph. 1:11; Prov. 16:4; Rom 11:36; 1 John 4:8, 16; Exod. 34:6-7; Heb. 11:6; Neh. 9:32-33; Psa. 5:5-6; Exod. 34:7; Nahum 1:2-3.

Is the above definition of God partial, or complete? Why do you think so?

_____
_____
_____
_____
_____

THE BEING OF GOD

God has a real, substantive existence. This is His *essence*. God is in His nature a substance (essence) which is infinite, eternal, and unchangeable. These, and other specifics about what we may know about God, are what we call His "attributes."

"There are many things belonging to the being of God, which we are not concerned to know, and which it would be a vain and bold curiosity to pry into but what is necessary to direct our practice, and tends to show how we should be towards him, is not (such has been his gracious granting), impossible or difficult to be known. We may apprehend him to be the most excellent Being; and may descend to many particular excellencies, in which we may easily apprehend him infinitely to surpass all other beings," (*Treatise on Delighting in God*).

John Howe (1630-1705)

What is Howe saying in the above quote? Place it in your own words.

_____
_____
_____
_____
_____

God's Divine Attributes

"Blessed be the LORD God of Israel from everlasting, and to everlasting. Amen, and Amen," (Psalm 41:13).

"Who is like unto the LORD our God, who dwelleth on high," (Psalm 113:5).

Concerning the divine essence, God has divine *perfections* called *attributes*. These are essential to the nature of God's divine *being*, and they are necessary in our idea about God. Attributes are divided into two classes: there are communicative attributes, and non-communicative attributes. Non-communicative attributes are those which we as human beings do not share, and that God has alone. God is negatively referred to in classes such as simplicity, infinity, eternity, and immutability. Communicative attributes are ones that we can experience, though God holds them in *His* being *perfectly*. Some of these are power, knowledge, holiness, justice, goodness, and truth. We are also able to classify the attributes of God as those referring to His essence (like infinity), those referring to His intellect (like knowledge), and those referring to His will (like justice).

{ "I am of the opinion, most aptly and as far as man's capacity is able to conceive that God may be defined this way, *that God is the first, most chief, and most perfect being from whom there flows and depends all entity and perfection.* For other things which are his attributes, as his eternity, his simplicity, his wisdom, and of like nature are all contained under this word of chief perfection," (*Treatise on the Knowledge of God*).

Peter Du Moulin (1568-1658) }

How is Du Moulin using the word, "perfection." What does that word mean in the context of studying the *Doctrine of God*?

_____
_____
_____
_____
_____

"Canst thou by searching find out God? canst thou find out the Almighty unto perfection?" (Job. 11:7). What does Job 11:7 mean concerning the word *perfection* in its context? Is it the same idea as Du Moulin's use of the word?

_____
_____
_____
_____
_____

In Job's use of the word and Du Moulin's use of the word is there a correlation to how we see God's "perfections" as his attributes? Can you explain how these two ideas merge into this idea of *God's being* having *perfections*?

_____
_____
_____
_____
_____
_____

INFINITY

The Bible says God is greater than that which can fill heaven and earth. 2 Chronicles 6:18 states, "But will God indeed dwell with men on the earth? behold, heaven and the heaven of heavens cannot contain thee; how much less this house which I have built!" God is exalted above all we can know or think.

Define what it means to be "infinite" without saying "not finite." Try to use another term or idea that will describe what being infinite means.

_____
_____
_____
_____
_____

When we say that God is *without limits* in His being and perfections, it means that *no limitation can be assigned to His essence.* For example, Psalm 147:5 relates God's essence to His knowledge and says, "Great is our Lord, and of great power: his understanding is infinite." This means that God's knowledge, if we are able to compartmentalize that one attribute, has no limits. God knows everything in every detail and in relationship to every other detail about everything. The student of Scripture can apply this idea of "without limits" to any of God's perfections.

Important Notation

A notation must be made about the idea that God is infinite. This does not mean that God *is* everything as the Pantheists teach. Pantheism teaches that God *is* the tree, *is* the rock, *is* the stars, *is* the created world, *etc.* God is infinite in His own nature, but that does not preclude that other entities He has created (which are finite) are part of Himself. They stand in *relation* to Himself, but are not *part* of Him. God as an infinite Spirit does not forbid the reality of the existence of something created. God exists as an infinite Spirit whose attributes have *no limits*. God is infinite in being because no limit can be assigned to His perfections. The created universe is not God and God is not the created universe. However, as we will see later, everything that exists, exists as a result of God's power to uphold the universe. This is not the same as God being the universe. Pantheism is a direct contradiction of Scripture, and of logic. There really are only two worldviews that one can hold, though there might be some derivations from those worldviews worked out in the way people think. Either you worship the universe and the things within it, *or*, you worship the infinite, triune God who made the universe, tells us about it in Scripture, and condescends to allow human beings to know him through his covenant with Jesus Christ. There are no other options on this. God is not the universe. He created it as a matrix for his own glory, for creaturely existence, and for the stage of his eternal plan through Jesus Christ for his elect saints.

Jonathan Edwards in his work on the *End of Creation* says that God's glory is, "...the emanation and true external expression of God's internal glory and fullness." God's glory includes, 1. "...the exercise of God's perfections to produce a proper effect," 2. "...the manifestation of his internal glory to created understandings," 3. "...the communication of the infinite fullness of God to the creature," and 4. "...the creature's high esteem of God, love to God, and complacence and joy in God; and the proper exercises and expressions of these," (*End of Creation*, Works, vol. 8, 527). The matrix of creation is the container in which these ideas take place.

In thinking about Edwards' deep ideas concerning God's glory, how does this help you understand the difference between *Christian theology concerning the nature of God*, and the way Pantheism teaches that *God is everything*?

_____

_____

_____

_____

_____

IMMENSITY

Infinity in relationship to *space* is called *immensity* or may be further termed omnipresence. God's *immensity* is the infinitude of His being in relationship to space. He fills immensity with His presence. His omnipresence is the infinitude of His being in relation *to His creatures*. He is equally present with all His creatures, at all times, and in all places.

Jacob said, "Surely the LORD is in this place; and I knew it not," (Gen. 28:16). God is not far from anyone. God fills all space. The limitations of space have no reference to Him. He is not absent from any portion of space, nor more present in one portion than in another. He is where He is in the fullness of His being always.

If God fills all space all the time, and there is no space where he is not infinitely present, what does that mean practically for you and your daily walk with Christ?

_____

_____

_____

_____

ETERNITY

What does it mean that God is at a perpetual rest and that there is no motions for him throughout the ages?

_____
_____
_____
_____

["Nothing exists from eternity but God, and God is not the matter or a part of any creature, but only the maker," (*The Marrow of Theology*).

William Ames (1576-1633)]

The infinitude of God relative to *duration* is His *eternity*. God is free from all the limitations of space *and time*. He does not exist during one period of time more than any another. For God all things are at an instantaneous *now*. There is no distinction between the present, past, and future.

["God's life is not a course of motions as ours, but a perpetual rest and in which there is no succession of parts," (*Treatise on the Knowledge of God*).

Peter Du Moulin (1568-1658)]

"Before the mountains were brought forth, or ever thou hadst formed the earth and the world, even from everlasting to everlasting thou art God," (Psalm 90:2). "Of old hast thou laid the foundation of the earth: and the heavens are the work of thy hands. They shall perish, but thou shalt endure: yea, all of them shall wax old like a garment; as a vesture shalt thou change them, and they shall be changed: but thou art the same, and thy years shall have no end," (Psalm 102:25-27). God is "the high and lofty One that inhabiteth eternity," (Isa. 57:15). For God, "a thousand years in thy sight are but as yesterday when it is past," (Psa. 90:4). And as the Apostle Peter echoes, "One day is with the Lord as a thousand years, and a thousand years as one day," (2 Pet. 3:8). Jesus Christ is, "the same yesterday, and today, and forever," (Heb. 13:8).

The Bible teaches that God is called the *eternal* or *everlasting* God. What does His primary designation in the Old Testament to His people as the great "I am" mean for this perfection?

_____
_____
_____
_____

Is God with Moses right now on the mountain delivering to him the 10 Commandments, while *at the same time* with David right now slaying Goliath, while *at the same time* right now with the apostle John on the Isle of Patmos, while *at the same time* with you here reading this workbook? Why or why not?

_____
_____
_____
_____

The Movie Clip

This will be a limited example of God's eternity, but hopefully it will help you answer the above question. Look at these frames of a movie film.

Let's assume you have the ability to look at all 4 frames at the same time. Unfortunately, we don't have the ability to optically look at the frames instantaneously as one, but for the purpose of the example, *pretend* you can. You would see 4 generations of a family. Each frame is successive and represents 40 years between each generation. Imagine for a moment that these 4 frames were actually expanded to 4,000,000 frames of everything that happened to these 4 generations and you had the ability to see them all *at the same time*. Imagine further that you had the ability to not only *see* the frames, but *interact* with them. In a certain way, the ½ dimension of time (which only moves forward in one direction) is not limiting the way

God sees or interacts with his created timeline. While he is here with you, the reader, in your present time, he is also with Moses on the mountain in Moses' time, and with David in his time, and with John in his time. Remember, God is not restricted by time or space. For us, we see the dimension of time in one forward view, (and we can speculate about how that time actually works, or wraps, or twists around in the space and time continuum). But for God, all time and space are present with him as an instantaneous point of "now." He does not move forward or back in time. He is always present with it. The Bible uses the term "eternal" for this.

How does the movie frame help you understand the way God sees interacts with creation?

___

Read Deuteronomy 33:27 and Ephesians 3:11.

IMMUTABILITY

The immutability of God is intimately connected with His immensity and eternity. We hear the Bible say, "He is the First and the Last," or "Alpha and Omega," or "the same yesterday, today and forever," or "They shall be changed, but thou art the same." God is exalted above even the *possibility* of change. Infinite space and infinite duration cannot change. They must forever be what they are. So God is absolutely immutable in His essence, and attributes and cannot change. He can neither increase nor decrease. He is not under any type of development, or evolution. His knowledge and power can never be greater or less than they are right now. He can never be more wise, holy, righteous or merciful than He ever has been and ever will be.

Why is God's immutability important for your own salvation?

___

James 1:17 says, He is, "the Father of lights, with whom is no variableness, neither shadow of turning." Numbers 23:19 states, "God is not a man that He should lie; neither the son of man that He should repent; hath He said and shall He not do it? or hath he spoken, and shall He not make it good?" One of my favorite passages is Isaiah 56:9-10, "I am God, and there is none like me, declaring the end from the beginning, and from ancient times the things that are not yet done, saying, My counsel shall stand, and I will do all my pleasure."

"When we think on God's unchangeableness let us consider *our own vanity* which is like a summer flower, we are so changeable, and seem so unlike God. To be one thing and then another thing is a property of a sinful and wretched man," (*Works of Hugh Binning*).

Hugh Binning (1627-1653)

 Read Malachi 3:6 and Genesis 6:6.

How do you reconcile these two ideas? On the one hand God does not change at all, which includes God changing His mind. On the other hand, Genesis 6 appears to say that God repents, which is changing his mind. Does God change or not?

_____
_____
_____
_____
_____

As a side note, there are some passages in Scripture in which God is said to *repent* (Gen 6:6, Exodus 32:14, Judges 2:18, 1 Samuel 15:35, Psalm 106:45, Amos 7:3, Amos 7:6, and Jonah 3:10) . These, though, are to be interpreted in the same way as those in which He is said to, ride upon the wings of the wind, hide people under His wings, save people by His "strong arm," or to, "walk through the earth." These create no difficulty and we will take some time to go over what that means in the section of the workbook dealing with God's decrees later on.

For now, consider those passages as *anthropomorphisms* which relate information about God to the intellect of the finite mind in a way that it can handle it. It will be a short excursus on God's decreed will and his perceptive will. (This topic is taken up extensively in my Ph.D. dissertation, *The Two Wills of God* and is *comprehensively* explained there, though it is theologically and philosophically *weighty*).

Sometimes rash theologians mix up immutability with immobility. In denying that God can change, they sometimes deny that He can *act*. Activity and immutability *are* compatible. God is able to relate without changing His character, will or attributes. He can wrestle with Jacob while continuing to be the immutable God.

List out five Bible verses that show God interacting in some way with people. With a cursory knowledge of the Bible, you should be able to do this quite easily. The only restriction is that you cannot use any Gospel passages concerning Jesus Christ's interaction in his incarnation. It would be too easy to simply say, "...all the verses in Matthew, Mark, Luke, John and Acts concerning Jesus." Instead, think through how God redemptively interacts and the key passages where those interactions may be cited.

_____
_____
_____
_____
_____
_____
_____

ASEITY, SIMPLICITY AND IMPASSABILITY

"God is independent, all sufficient in Himself, and the only source of all existence and life. YHWH is the name that describes this essence and identity most clearly: "I will be what I will be." It is in this aseity of God, conceived not only as having being from himself but also as the fullness of being, that all other divine perfections are included," (*Reformed Dogmatics* Volume 2).

Herman Bavinck (1854-1921)

What does it mean that God is all-sufficient and independent concerning His *being*?

_____
_____
_____
_____
_____

"God *hath life* in himself: He is the "living God", therefore "steadfast forever," (Dan 6:26). He hath life by his essence, not by participation. He is the sun to give light and life to all creatures, but receives not light or life from anything, and therefore he hath an unlimited life; not a drop of life, but a fountain; not a spark of a limited life, but a life transcending all bounds. He hath life in Himself; all creatures have their life in Him and from Him," (*The Works of Stephen Charnock*, Volume 1).

Stephen Charnock (1626-1680)

What does it mean that God *hath life in himself?*

_____
_____
_____
_____
_____

God is self-existent and has the power of necessary being. This is theologically called "aseity". The word "aseity" comes from the Latin meaning, "from the self." God alone has the power of being in and of Himself. Necessary being is extremely important in the way we understand the universe. If *something* exists, then "something" exists *necessarily*. This attribute belongs to the group of the incommunicable attributes of God like immutability and being infinite. God *alone* has the power of being. He is able, from nothing, to create something, as He did when fashioning the world. "In the beginning God created the heaven and the earth," (Gen. 1:1). Aseity further implies divine *simplicity*. God is a necessary *single* being which has *no parts* of any kind. He has no spatial parts, no temporary parts and no abstract parts. I have arms and legs. I have a brain, eyes, and a liver. I am made up of *parts*. God is *spirit*, and simple. He has no parts whatsoever. When I lay on my couch my head is at one end and my feet are at another. In differentiation, God is simple. He is one being who has His entire being in every place. He is in the fullness of His being. He is necessarily there in His entirety.

> "We can conceive no other of God, if he were not a pure, entire unmixed Spirit," (*Existence and Attributes of God*, Volume 1).
> Stephen Charnock (1626-1680)

What do you think Charnock meant when he said "unmixed spirit?"

_____
_____
_____
_____

A further implication of God's constitution as a necessary and simple being with no parts is that He is without emotion or is "impassible." Emotion implies standing in relation to some external agent. Emotion implies *dependence*. For example, a person acts in a certain way and another person reacts to that first person. That is dependence. God is not dependent on any person or thing.

 Read Psalm 102:11 and 1 Peter 1:24.

We are like grass that withers. Even our "glory" is despicable. How dependent are you on other "things?" Can you name a few "things, people, etc." that you are dependent on?

_____
_____
_____
_____

Since God has created *everything*, He is not dependent on His creation *ever*. The Scriptural "emotions" that are given to God as being angry, loving, jealous, *etc.* are *anthropomorphisms* which are given in *relation* to the subject, not the *disposition* of the object. Let me use a simple example. Walk outside tonight when the moon is full and look at the moon head on. Stare at it. You stand in relation to the moon. Then turn around with the moon to your back. Now you stand in a *different* relation to the moon. The moon hasn't changed. *You have*. Your relationship with the moon changed. To *you*, the moon is in a different place with a different *effect* on you. To the moon, *nothing has changed*. The Scriptural expressions of anger, love, *etc.* are *relational* to *men*, not changes in God's *disposition* or *character*. In this way God is a necessary being, who is without passions or parts. God never changes; men do in relation to Him.

Thomas Aquinas got a number of theological things "wrong" overall in his systematic theology. However, we find him often correct on a number of key issues, one of which is God's impassability. Aquinas argues that God cannot change, and rightly so. He says in 89:1 of the *Summa Contra Gentiles*, titled, *That in God there are not the passions of the appetites*, he says, "But in God there *are* delight and joy, but they are not opposed to the divine perfection."

How can you explain that God does not change, and yet has joy and delight?

_____
_____
_____
_____
_____

["To conceive God or the Trinity as mutable and passable is to proffer a relationship with creatures that is literally impotent and thoroughly impoverished," (*Works of John Owen*, 12:110).
John Owen (1616-1683)]

If God could change, how would that make our relationship to him "impoverished" as Owen says?

_____
_____
_____
_____
_____

> "But to God nothing of this sort occurs; for He is neither deceived, nor does He deceitfully promise anything, nor, as James says, is there with Him any "shadow of turning." (James 1:7.) We now understand to what this dissimilitude between God and men refers, namely, that we should not travesty God according to our *own* notions, but, in our consideration of His nature, should remember that he is liable to no changes, since He is far above all heavens." (*Commentary on Numbers* 23:19).
>
> John Calvin (1509-1564)

How do Christians often "travesty God" (to use Calvin's words) by making their own notions of God? What affect does this have on the Christian, and his Christian walk?

_____
_____
_____
_____
_____

GOD IS ALL-KNOWING (OMNISCIENT) AND EVERYWHERE PRESENT (OMNIPRESENT)

God knows everything in an instantaneous *now*. He does not think forward, or remember back. He knows everything right now, always. God is seen in Scripture as the ever present eye to which all things are perfectly revealed. Even those things which seem mundane, like the individual follicles of hair on our head are all known by God.

 Read Hebrews 4:13, Psalm 139:1-2, Proverbs 15:3, and Matt. 10:30.

God knows all things as they are, being as being, phenomena as phenomena, the possible as possible, the actual as actual, the necessary as necessary, the free as free, the past as past, the present as present, the future as future, although all things are ever present in His view.

["We know God sees all things, yet we live and walk as if He knows nothing," (*Works*, Volume 1).
Stephen Charnock (1626-1680)]

Is Charnock right? How is this true in your own life?
_____
_____
_____
_____
_____

How can you improve being reminded of God's all-seeing eye in your own life?
_____
_____
_____
_____
_____

The Reformed Apprentice Volume 3: The Doctrine of God

{ "Is God so infinite in knowledge? Then we should *always* feel as under His omniscient eye," (*Body of Divinity*).
Thomas Watson (1620-1686) }

To use the term anthropomorphically, what do you think God sees *more of*? Circle those that you think God *really* takes notice of...

(a) any sin   (b) any good work   (c) only heinous sins   (d) a minister's sermon
(e) the Christian's prayer life   (f)   white lies   (g) course joking   (h) godly conversation
(i) the thoughts of the wicked   (j)   the thoughts of the righteous   (k) deeds of great men
(l) the life of a beggar   (m)   our bible reading   (n) the way we treat animals

{ "God knows every man and woman that ever was, or shall be, God knows them before they are. God knows all the ways and works of men, from the birth, and from the womb. God knows all the speeches of all men. God knows not only the ways and the words, but even the thoughts of men. God knows all the ways, words, and thoughts of men present and past, so he knows all the ways, words, and thoughts of men that are to come. This knowledge which God has of all things, is clear and distinct. All things are naked," (*The All-Seeing Unseen Eye of God and Other Sermons*).
Matthew Newcomen (1610-1669) }

What does Newcomen mean when he says that all things are "naked" before God?

_____
_____
_____
_____

The omniscience of God also follows from His omnipresence. God is everywhere present in the fullness of His being at all times.

Is God in hell? Why or why not?

_____
_____
_____
_____

> "*Hell* in Scripture is called "wrath to come." 1 Thessalonians 1:10, "He hath delivered us from the wrath to come," that is, from hell. And the reason why hell is called *wrath to come* is to show that it is the *wrath of God* that makes hell *to be hell*. If it were possible for a man to have the favor of God in hell, hell would be a heaven to him; but the lack of the favor of God makes hell to be hell," (*Treatise on Hell*).
>
> Christopher Love (1618-1651)

God is as fully present *in hell* as He is in heaven. There is no place anywhere where God is not. As God fills heaven *and* earth, all things are happening in His presence. He knows our thoughts far better than they are known to ourselves. When we lust, He knows it. He is present there at the time we are lusting. When we pray, He knows it. He is there at the time we pray and knew before we prayed what we would pray and how well we would pray it, or how poorly we would pray. When we lie, He knows it. He both knows it and is present at the transaction of all occurrences of all things for all time. In this way, omnipresence and omniscience allow God to justly judge all things by His righteous character as moments occur in this forward dimension of time.

Explain the difference between Pantheism and Christian Theology concerning God's presence? How is God everywhere present, but yet not the tree, or the cat?

_____
_____
_____
_____
_____

THE WISDOM OF GOD

Wisdom and knowledge are obviously intimately related. Wisdom manifests itself in the selection of proper ends and means for the accomplishment of God's glory. For example, as nature shows a specific design, so all the works of God demonstrate His wisdom. This occurs from the minutest movement of a grain of sand shifting on the beach, to the means accomplishing the particular end of salvation for the manifestation of His own glory. When we worship God, we call on Him saying, "The only wise God...O Lord, how manifold are thy works! in wisdom hast Thou made them all," (Psa. 104:24). Even Paul said, "O! the depth of the riches both of the wisdom and knowledge of God!" (Rom. 11:33.).

Have you ever had a time in your life that you *disliked* the providence of God at some point of your walk, or job, or situation in life?
YES   NO

How does that "dislike" impinge on God's wisdom, or your understanding of God's wisdom as it relates to his glory?

_____
_____
_____
_____
_____

THE WILL OF GOD

God has a will that demonstrates itself in both power and purpose. God wills His own actions necessarily, and the actions outside of Himself freely. God is a voluntary agent with the power of self-determination. The Bible speaks of the will of God in His decrees, purposes, counsels, and commands. God's will is free in the highest sense of the word. He acts according to His own pleasure, according to His own sense of what is wise, right, or desirable. He is free in acting, creating, and preserving all things.

What is God's will for your life?

_____
_____
_____
_____
_____

What is God's *preceptive will* for your life? (This should be *easy*.)

_____
_____
_____
_____
_____

What is God's *decretive will* for your life? (This one is *tricky*.)

_____
_____
_____
_____
_____

There is a difference between the *decretive* will of God and the *preceptive* will of God. The decretive will of God concerns His purposes, and relates to the futurition of events that God determines will happen before they actually happen in time. He plans them. For example, God wills the salvation of a particular person which He will provide all the means for that saving act to come to pass. But we have no idea what God's decretive will entails. We can see things after the fact, but not before the fact. For example, it was God's will that Joseph be sold into slavery. God decreed this though it was a violation of the 5th and sixth commandments, and others. The preceptive will relates to the rule of duty for His rational creatures for all time. For example, the Law of God in the Ten Commandments demonstrates what all men should do. Both of these encompass God's will.

Which one applies to what *you can know* – God's decreed will or his preceptive will? (This is *tricky too*.)

_____
_____
_____
_____
_____

These two aspects of His will are never in conflict. He *permits* men to sin, although sin is *forbidden*. God also *commands* men to accomplish things they can never fulfill *without His help*. As Christ says, "Unless a man *is* born again he *cannot* see..." God may command men to repent and believe, and yet, for wise reasons unknown to us, He may abstain from giving them the ability of repentance through the power of the Holy Spirit (John 3:1-10). Why? This is God's secret will. By the secret will of God, is meant, His purposes as hidden in His own mind. God's revealed will are His precepts and His purposes made known to His creatures in His word which they are to follow. The will of God is the ultimate ground of moral obligation to all rational creatures. But not all rational creatures may be given the ability to successfully fulfill God's commands, precepts, statutes and laws. From the simple to the complex, God decrees and allows occurrences throughout all time. Jeremiah 5:22 states, "Fear ye not me? saith the LORD: will ye not tremble at my presence, which have placed the sand for the bound of the sea *by a perpetual decree*, that it cannot pass it: and though the waves thereof toss themselves, yet can they not prevail; though they roar, yet can they not pass over it?" At the same time, God commands certain ends for men based on their actions in response to His law, "And the LORD said unto Moses, Whosoever hath sinned against me, him will I blot out of my book," (Exod. 32:33). Thus, every Christian should hold fast to the preceptive will of God in His word, "Thy word have I hid in mine heart, that I might not sin against thee," (Psa. 119:11).

> "(1) Every decree of God is eternal; therefore it cannot depend upon a condition which takes place only in time. (2) God's decrees depend on his good pleasure (*eudokia*) (Mt. 11:26; Eph. 1:5; Rom. 9:11). Therefore they are not suspended upon any condition outside of God. (3) Every decree of God is immutable (Is. 46:10; Rom. 9:11)," (*Institutes of Elenctic Theology*, Volume 1).
> Francis Turretin (1623-1687)

God's decrees are not conditional on any "things." What does Turretin mean by that, and also by saying that God's decrees are accomplished solely according to His good pleasure?

_____
_____
_____
_____
_____

Find 5 verses that demonstrate the "eternal" and "immutable" nature of God's decrees?

_____
_____
_____
_____
_____

OMNIPOTENCE

Omnipotence is power without limits. The word comes from the Latin designation – complete power or *all-power*. When we remove all limitations concerning "power" we have God's omnipotence in view. In this sense, God can *do* whatever He *wills*. God wills and it is done. In the beginning He said, "Let there be light; *and there was light*." Jesus Christ did the same. He caused the winds to cease and there was a great calm. He healed the sick, opened the eyes of the blind, and raised the dead by His own will and word. We call God, in this way, "almighty." He has *all-*might.

 Read Genesis 12:1, Jer. 32:17, and Psa. 115:3.

God is all powerful. Atheists often like to play games with questions concerning Christian beliefs. Here is one that is often cited: Can God create a rock that is too big for Him to lift?

How do you adequately answer that "atheistical" question?

_____
_____
_____
_____
_____

Is there a limitation to God's power? There is a no limitation to God's power, but there is a limitation to God's effects of power. This concerns a reference to the production of *possible* effects. For example, God cannot do what is *impossible*. But is it not said that with God "all things" are possible? Taken in context, yes, all things concerning the *salvation of men* are possible with God. The text says, "But Jesus beheld them, and said unto them, With men *this* is impossible; but with God all things are possible," (Matt. 19:26). "This" pertains to that which accompanies the transformation in salvation. "Who then can be saved?" God can save. All things pertaining to salvation with God in control are possible. However, God cannot create a *square circle* because a square circle is against reason and logic. Square circles cannot exist. In this way, God cannot perform the *illogical*. That would be contrary to God's nature. We must remember that God's will is determined by His nature. There is no actual limitation to perfection to say that *God cannot be imperfect*. God will always be perfect and cannot negate His nature. Such is the case with the rock too big for God to lift, *etc*. It violates logic.

"Divine power is limited *only* by the absurd and self-contradictory. God can do anything that does not imply a logical impossibility. A logical impossibility means that the predicate is contradictory to the subject; for example, a material spirit, a corporeal deity, a sensitive stone, an irrational man, a body without parts or extension, a square triangle. These are not objects of power, and therefore it is really no limitation of divine omnipotence to say that it cannot create them. They involve the absurdity that a thing can be and not be at the same time. A logical impossibility is, in truth, a nonentity; and to say that God cannot create a nonentity is not a limitation or denial of power. For power is the ability to create entity," (*Reformed Dogmatics*).

W.G.T. Shedd (1820-1894)

"God's omnipotence may be defined as His ability to do *all things*,"

(*Systematic Theology*).

R.L. Dabney (1820-1898)

If we limited "all things" to God's omnipotent nature, is there *anything* God cannot do?

_____
_____
_____
_____
_____

📖 Read Habakkuk 1:13. Is there anything God cannot do?   YES   NO

How does this apply to God's omniscience? If He cannot look on evil, how can He judge evil? How do you explain this?

_____
_____
_____
_____
_____

THE HOLINESS OF GOD

We move from incommunicable attributes to communicable. These attributes are those we can share with God, or rather reflect of God, but do not possess them perfectly. The first is holiness. When we say God is "holy" it refers to the moral perfection of God's nature. God is morally perfect and cannot "do" evil.

📖 Read 1 Samuel 2:2, Psalm 99:9, Psalm 111:9.

Define the word, "holy," and use two Scriptures to defend your definition.

_____
_____
_____
_____
_____

God is holy in that He is completely free from moral evil. He is also holy in that He is utterly morally perfect. God is free from any type of impurity, or any type of transgression of His holy Law. God does not transgress His Law, nor is He ever in want of conformity to His Law.

Men must be cleansed from evil. This is where we get the idea of "sanctification" as "cleansing."

 Read Isaiah 6.

God is so holy and so morally separate from evil that the seraphim's (His angels) are set around His throne to continue, day and night, saying, "Holy, Holy, Holy is the Lord God Almighty." In comparison to God's holiness, men are *evil*. Even the best works of men are as filthy rags in comparison to God's nature. This is why Isaiah exclaimed, "Woe is me! for I am undone; because I am a man of unclean lips, and I dwell in the midst of a people of unclean lips: for mine eyes have seen the king, the Lord of hosts," (Isa. 6:5.).

> "*Holiness* is that which beareth the bell, and maketh the music in the ears of God. And if the sound thereof be not heard before the Lord, we shall surely die," (*Of Holiness*).
> John Sheffield (?-1680)

> "God's nature is essentially holy, by which he cannot have communion with any one that is unholy, no more than light can have "fellowship with darkness;" but he indispensably hates and opposes all wickedness, and hath declared his enmity against it. As fire cannot but devour stubble, so God's holiness will not suffer him to spare any whom he finds sin and guilt upon," (*The Believer's Dignity and Duty*).
> Peter Vinke (?-1702)

God knows that we as human beings think in *parts* and *pieces*. In talking about God we have to break down ideas we have about Him to apprehend different aspects of Him, though He is one simple being *without* passions or parts. The Bible compartmentalizes ideas about God to us so we can apprehend Him. Uniquely, Scripture ascribes *holiness* to all God's attributes. In God's anger, He has a holy anger. In God's justice, He has a holy justice. In God's love, He has a holy love. All His attributes throughout Scripture have a correlation and emphasis *to us* as being holy. Yes, God is infinitely lovely, and immutably just, and omnipotently angry. But the Bible places a special emphasis on God's separation from moral evil where this "central" attribute of holiness takes up much of the Bible's description of God. This is worthy of the student's notation about the character of God and our relationship to Him as sinful, fallen creatures.

{ "*The holiness of God is a self-holiness.*—God is not only full, but self-full, full with his own fullness: he lends to all, borrows of none," (*What is That Fullness of God Every True Christian Ought to Pray and Strive to Be Filled With?*)
Vincent Alsop (1630-1703). }

What does Alsop mean when he says that "God is self-full" of holiness?

_____
_____
_____
_____
_____

{ "*Lament the loss of holiness.*—We may complain that holiness is lost and fallen in the streets. Some complain of loss of trade: "In these sad times trade is dead: there is no trade:" we may say this trade is lost or dead, there is little holiness stirring," (*Of Holiness*).
John Sheffield (?-1680) }

JUSTICE

The word justice, or righteousness, is used in Scripture in a moral sense to mean "right." The Hebrew idea behind speaking of God's righteousness is speaking of God's "rightness." The Greek idea in the New Testament links that idea with its negation of "missing the mark." When someone misses the mark, or sins, they are being unrighteous. When men conform to what is right in a moral sense they imitate God. God is a righteous Ruler who has Laws that are holy, just and good. God faithfully adheres to those Laws as consistent with His nature. Men are to do the same. God judges according to His nature, and according to His holiness. "God is a righteous judge," (Psa. 7:11). "He shall judge the world with righteousness," (Ps. 96:13). The Psalmist also writes, "Clouds and darkness are round about Him: righteousness and judgment are the habitation of his throne," (Psa. 97:2).

"God is a being infinitely lovely, because he hath infinite excellency and beauty. To have infinite excellency and beauty, is the same thing as to have infinite loveliness. He is a being of infinite greatness, majesty, and glory; and therefore he is infinitely honorable. He is infinitely exalted above the greatest potentates of the earth, and highest angels in heaven; and therefore he is infinitely more honorable than they. His authority over us is infinite; and the ground of his right to our obedience is infinitely strong; for he is infinitely worthy to be obeyed himself, and we have an absolute, universal, and infinite dependence upon him. So that sin against God, being a violation of infinite obligations, must be a crime infinitely heinous, and so deserving of infinite punishment," (*The Justice of God in the Damnation of Sinners*).

Jonathan Edwards (1703-1758)

God always does what is right. His nature dictates that proposition. Edwards explained that because God's nature is infinitely perfect in every way, when someone sins against Him, God in His justice must punish sin infinitely. Is this actually just or not? Should a finite sin, that lasts only a moment or two, be punished for eternity? Why or why not?

_____
_____
_____
_____
_____

How did Edwards rightly apply God's infinite justice on a momentary sin in the last sentence of the quote above?

_____
_____
_____
_____
_____

Read Deut. 32:4.

If God always acts justly against wickedness, and always righteously judges in accordance with His holy nature, how are sinful fallen men *able* to be saved?

_____
_____
_____
_____
_____

THE GOODNESS OF GOD

The goodness of God is something most secularized churches harp upon, and not to their shame. It's wonderful that people look to the goodness of God and praise God for it. It's not so good if they don't know what it means that "God is good." Generally, the secularized church gets their theology from songs by people like Velna Ledin who wrote a song called "God is so Good" in 1933, about the time that pithy praise songs started to gain momentum. Here are the complete lyrics to the song:

> *God is so good,*
> *God is so good,*
> *God is so good,*
> *He's so good to me!*

The "song" is based on 1 Chronicles 16:34, "O give thanks unto the Lord, for He is good," and was composed to "pass the time on a road trip." Is this akin to 99 bottles of beer on the wall? That was used to pass time as well. What does this song mean?

Or how about the child's prayer.

> *God is Great, God is Good;*
> *Let us thank Him for our food.*
> *By His hands we all are fed,*
> *Give us Lord our Daily Bread.*

Without having a context and a teaching, these mean little, though they are true. Yet, not only do they mean little, but they are *reversed* in their theological explanations. From the way the song is written, or the prayer is prayed, God is so good because *he is so good to me, or gives me food*. But God is good because he is full of His own goodness, not simply because he is good to me. If we minimize the song or prayer, they simply say, "God is so good to me." But that is not why God is good. If nothing existed other than God, as it was before creation, God was still good.

> "Goodness is the very opposite of harshness, cruelty, gruffness, severity, mercilessness—all of which are far removed from God," (*The Christian's Reasonable Service*).
> Wilhelm a'Brakel (1635-1711)

God is good because His nature is good. Further, goodness is a combination of and includes benevolence, love, mercy, and grace. By benevolence, is meant God's disposition to 1) promote His own happiness and then 2) the happiness of His creatures. Mercy is kindness exercised towards the miserable. Grace is love exercised towards the unworthy. This is a most incredible doctrine. The object of God's love is *Christ* in men. It is no mystery to see that God hates men and hates sin in men. "Jacob have I loved, but Esau have I hated," (Rom 9:13). It is most mysterious and incredible that God *loves Christ in men* in loving His church. *Sinners* are *loved* by God in this way. Amazing. According to His will, God saves sinners, "That in the ages to come He might show the exceeding riches of his grace in his kindness toward us, through Christ Jesus," (Eph. 2:7).

The goodness of God also has a general nature in reference to all God's creatures.

Read Psalm 33:5, Matthew 5:45 and Lamentations 3:25.
If God is good to all, how is He good to the wicked?

_____
_____
_____
_____
_____

The goodness of God in the form of benevolence is revealed in nature where we see life teeming with enjoyment. Love to the undeserving demonstrates benevolence. This also moves into the realm of redemption and God's purpose for His people. "For God so loved the world, that He gave his only begotten Son, that whosoever believeth in Him should not perish, but have everlasting life," (John 3:16). The Apostle John also said, "Herein is love, not that we loved God, but that He loved us, and sent his Son to be the propitiation for our sins," (1 John 4:10). This benevolent love of God includes delight in its object (as a result of being joined with Christ) with the desire of possession and communion. God is love and love in Him is, in all that is essential to its nature, what love is in us. In this the Christian should rejoice exceedingly. The infinite God of the universe *condescended to love men*.

> "Without due apprehensions and conceptions of God, we cannot perform any part of that natural worship we owe to God.—We cannot love him, fear him, trust in him, pray unto him, praise him, *etc.*," (*How We May Have Suitable Conceptions of God*).
> Thomas Mallery (1605-1671)

If our understanding of God as good is misguided, how will that affect the way we love Him, trust Him, pray, *etc.*?

_____
_____
_____
_____
_____

Knowing God is good in and of Himself, what are two of the greatest expressions of God's goodness to His creatures? Use Scripture to prove them.

_____
_____
_____
_____
_____

Listen to one of the Westminster Divines (John Gibbon (1587-n.d.). on the further demonstration of God's goodness. "*The free grace of God* is the first wheel that sets all the rest in motion. Its contribution is that of a first cause, or internal motive, disposing God to send his Son, (John 3:16,) that sinners, believing, might be "justified freely by his grace through the redemption that is in Christ Jesus." (Rom. 3:24.) For Christ died not to render God good; (he was so eternally;) but that, with the honor of his justice, he might exert and *display his goodness*, which contrived and made itself this way to break forth into the world," (*The Nature of Justification Opened*).

How does God display His goodness in the Covenant of Grace most effectively?

_____
_____
_____
_____

THE TRUTH OF GOD

The truth of God is the foundation of all religion. It is the ground of the Christian's assurance so that what God has revealed of Himself and of His will, in His works and in the Scriptures, may be *relied* upon. Moses records in Deuteronomy 32:4, "He is the Rock, his work is perfect: for all his ways are judgment: *a God of truth* and without iniquity, just and right is he." Christ said through the Holy Spirit guiding the Apostles, "Even the Spirit of truth; whom the world cannot receive, because it seeth him not, neither knoweth him: but ye know him; for he dwelleth with you, and shall be in you," (John 14:17).

Pontius Pilate said to Christ, "What is truth?" How would you define truth in your own words? And how does "truth" apply to God's character?

_____
_____

_____

_____

_____

{ "We must pray that God would establish his Church in truth," (*The All-Seeing Unseen Eye of God and Other Sermons*).
Matthew Newcomen (1610-1669) }

"Heretics make churches, but they are void of truth which is that sweet honey that is to be found only among the faithful," William Spurstowe (1605-1666). Why is, "establishing God's church in truth," over and against the practices of "heretics," important in relation to the *attributes* of God?

_____

_____

_____

_____

_____

The third commandment teaches us that we ought not to take the name of the Lord in vain. God's name and His word are closely related because keeping God's word means honoring His name. Listen to Thomas Watson on this point, "When in any way we profane and abuse his word. The word of God is profaned, in general, when profane men meddle with it. It is unseemly and unbecoming a wicked man to talk of sacred things, of God's providence, and the decrees of God and heaven. It was very distasteful to Christ to hear the devil quote Scripture, "It is written." To hear a wicked man who wallows in sin talk of God and religion is offensive; it is taking God's name in vain. When the word of God is in a drunkard's mouth, it is like a pearl hung upon a swine. Under the law, the lips of the leper were to be covered. (Leviticus 13:45). The lips of a profane, drunken minister ought to be covered; he is unfit to speak God's word, because he takes his name in vain," (*Ten Commandments*).

Since God's name is so closely related to His word, and His word reflects His attributes and being, how well should we know God's word? And if we know more of the word of God, how does that help our conceptions of God's attributes in relation to "truth?"

_____
_____
_____
_____

> "Truth is seated in the understanding, and speaks the Spirit's leading of that faculty: holiness reaches to the heart within, and conversation without; and speaks the Spirit's leading of both, in their utmost comprehensiveness," (*The Leading of the Holy Spirit Opened*).
>
> Thomas Jacomb (1622-1687).

How are we led by the Holy Spirit to hold steadfast to the truth? What is Jacomb in the above quote explaining, and how does this apply to God's attributes which include "truth?"

_____
_____
_____
_____

THE SOVEREIGNTY OF GOD

If there was any attribute so utterly abused in our day, and in the day of the Reformation, it was, understanding the sovereignty of God. Sovereignty is an *ability* arising out of the perfections of God's Supreme *Being*. If God is infinite, eternal, all-powerful and immutable in

His being and perfections, He has every right (*necessarily*) to exercise absolute sovereignty.

Read Psalm 115:8, Daniel 4:35, and Psalm 24:1.

Is God sovereign over your life? Why or why not? Give some examples.

_____
_____
_____
_____
_____

God even assumes right of possession in Scripture when He says, "Behold, all souls are mine; as the soul of the father, so also the soul of the son is mine." (Ezek. 18:4). And Christ says the same when he remarks, "Is it not lawful for me to do what I will with mine own?" (Matt. 20:15). God's sovereignty is universal, absolute and immutable. He exercises it in establishing laws, determining the nature of created beings, and even appoints each individual his position and lot in life.

Is God sovereign over the salvation of your relatives? Why or why not? Give some examples.

_____
_____
_____
_____
_____

Is God's sovereignty contentious for you, or something that is a comfort? Explain. Give some examples.

_____
_____
_____

Define, in your own words, "sovereign control."

Is there anything in the created universe that is out of God's sovereign control? What examples do some people use of God *not* being sovereign over everything?

At this point, we are not going to delve into sovereignty *and salvation*, the *ordo salutis*, etc. That will be covered in another workbook.

THE EXISTENCE OF EVIL

If God is all-powerful, all-knowing, and filled with love, what do we do with "evil?" How can the existence of evil be reconciled with the benevolence and holiness of a God infinite in wisdom and power? Couldn't God simply stop evil from coming into being? First, we might rest with the assurance that the Judge of all the earth must and will do right. Evil exists because God *decreed* that it should. Without evil, His church would never know the love of the Savior. Sin and the fall of Adam in the garden then becomes a necessary means of the greatest *good*.

Is there such a thing as *ultimate* evil? Why or why not?

_____
_____
_____
_____
_____

Though God could have created a world without sin, or the allowance of the fall, God in His wisdom saw the existence of sin and evil as a proper means to His glorified end. The glory of God is the end to which the promotion of holiness, and the production of happiness, and all other ends are subordinate. We must, then be content that the only wise God planned for sin in such a way *as to bring Him the most glory*. This is what Paul meant when he said in Romans 9:22, "What if God, willing to show his wrath, and to make his power known, endured with much long suffering the vessels of wrath fitted to destruction: and that He might make known the riches of his glory on the vessels of mercy, which He had afore prepared unto glory." Sin is permitted that the justice of God may be known in its punishment, and His grace in its forgiveness. We should rest satisfied that a universe constructed by God for the purpose of making Himself known is a far better universe than one designed for the production of mere creature happiness.

The Trinity

Matthew 28:19, "Go ye therefore, and teach all nations, baptizing them in the name of the Father, and of the Son, and of the Holy Ghost."

 Read Genesis 1:1, 1:26 and 3:22.

What observations can you see in these verses that point to God being more than one person?

_____
_____
_____
_____
_____

The doctrine of the Trinity is a teaching found *only* in the Bible. First, note must be made that there is one God and one God only to be worshipped. Scripture says that there is only one living and true God, or divine Being. Deuteronomy 6:4 states, "The Lord our God is one Lord." Isaiah records, "I am the first, and I am the last; and besides me there is no God," (Isa. 54:6). The Apostle James says, "Thou believest that there is one God; thou doest well," (James 2:19). The Ten Commandments teach us (in God's top 10 laws men must know) "Thou shalt have no other gods before me."

Secondly, the Bible equally ascribes all divine titles and attributes of God to the Father, Son, and Spirit. Listen to what Hodge says here about the Trinity.

> "The same divine worship is rendered to them. The one is as much the object of adoration, love, confidence, and devotion as the other. It is not more evident that the Father is God, or that the Son is God; nor is the deity of the Father and Son more clearly revealed than that of the Spirit," (*Systematic Theology*).
>
> Charles Hodge (1797-1878)

Thirdly, the terms Father, Son, and Spirit do not express different relations of God to His creatures as modalism teaches (one God with three different masks) otherwise called Sabellianism. Sabellianism teaches *one* God with three different masks depending on what he is doing at the time.

Father	Son	Spirit
Old Testament	New Testament	Present

In contrast to the Sabellian heresy, there is *one* divine *Being* which subsists in *three persons*, Father, Son, and Spirit. The non-contradictory manner in which we understand the Scriptural teaching runs along this line of thought: 1) There is one divine Being. 2) The Father, Son, and Spirit are divine. 3) The Father, Son, and Spirit are distinct persons. 4) The Father, Son, and Spirit possess the same attributes and are the same in substance. 5) Being the same in substance, they are equal in power and glory. *One God in three persons.*

> "All the world now should never make me doubt of the Triune God in unity," (*Directions for the Private Reading of the Scriptures*).
> Nicholas Byfield (1579-1622)

"I and my Father are one," (Joh. 10:30). Though the Father, Son, and Spirit are the same in *substance*, equal in power and glory, it is also true that there is a specific way in which we perceive their *actions*. The Father is first, the Son second, and the Spirit third. The Son is of the Father, and the Spirit is of the Father and of the Son. The Father sends the Son, and the Father and Son send the Spirit. The Father operates through the Son, and the Father and Son operate through the Spirit. In the Trinity, then, according to Scripture, there is a subordination of the Persons as to the mode of *operation*.

Read Genesis 1:1, John 1:1ff, and Col. 1:16 concerning the work of the Spirit and the Son.

The Trinity is credited with the creation of the world *equally*. The Father created the world, the Son created the world, and the Spirit created the world. Some precise variations are also mentioned in their operation. The Father preserves all things; the Son upholds all things; and the Spirit is the source of all life. There are also some acts which are precisely referred to the Father, others to the Son, and others to the Spirit. The Father creates, elects, and draws, the Son redeems, and the Spirit sanctifies.

Use a concordance: find one Scripture for each person demonstrating that the Father preserves all things; the Son upholds all things; and the Spirit is the source of all life.

_____
_____
_____

Lastly, there is what we call in theology a "mode of subsisting" for the Trinity. This is the manner in which Scripture teaches us the existence of the Trinity, and in specific actions that the persons of the Trinity act from one another. *Generation* belongs exclusively to the Father, *filiation* to the Son, and *procession* to the Spirit.

Scripture shows us that there is one God in three persons. The names of God are in the plural form, "Let us make man in our image," (Gen. 1:26). "Let us go down, and there confound their language, that they may not understand one another's speech. So the LORD scattered them abroad from thence upon the face of all the earth: and they left off to build the city," (Gen. 11:7-8). There is a distinction made between Yahweh (the great I AM), and the angel of the Lord to whom all divine titles are given, and divine worship is rendered. "The angel of the LORD encampeth round about them that fear him, and delivereth them," (Psa. 34:7). In the Trinitarian formula of baptism Christians are baptized in the, "name of the Father, of the Son, and of the Holy Spirit," (Matthew 28:19). In the Apostolic Benediction a prayer is addressed to Christ for His grace, to the Father for His love, and to the Spirit for His fellowship. "The grace of the Lord Jesus Christ, and the love of God, and the communion of the Holy Ghost, be with you all. Amen," (2 Cor. 13:14).

ETERNAL GENERATION OF THE SON & THE PROCESSION OF THE HOLY SPIRIT

The Son is *eternally generated* of the Father. This generation is said to be an eternal movement in the divine essence. This is by necessity of nature. It does not involve any separation or division in the Godhead, and it is without change. The chief text supporting this is the passage in John 5:26, "As the Father hath life in Himself, so hath He given to the Son to have life in Himself." The relationship between the First and Second persons in the Trinity is expressed by the words *Father* and *Son*. This simply demonstrates that there is a communication of the essence of the Godhead from the Father to the Son in the Holy Trinity. Consequently, every time the Scriptures call Jesus the Son of God, they assert His true and proper divinity. The Apostle John says, "And I saw, and bare record that this is the Son of

God," (John 1:34). In his epistle to the churches John later says, "And we know that the Son of God is come, and hath given us an understanding, that we may know him that is true, and we are in him that is true, even in his Son Jesus Christ. This is the true God, and eternal life," (1 John 5:20). This gives way to the term "only begotten". Christ is declared to be, "the only-begotten Son of God," "His own Son," *i.e.*, His Son in a peculiar and proper sense. John 1:14 states, "And the Word was made flesh, and dwelt among us, (and we beheld his glory, the glory as of the only begotten of the Father,) full of grace and truth."

The Spirit proceeds from the Father *and* Son. This is the communication of essence from the Father and the Son eternally to the Spirit. The Third Person of the Trinity is called *Spirit* because of His relation to the First and Second persons of the Trinity. Jesus taught that *He* sends the Spirit, and that the Spirit *also* proceeds from the Father, "But when the Comforter is come, whom *I* will send unto you *from* the Father, even the Spirit of truth, which proceedeth from the Father, he shall testify of me," (John 15:26). The Spirit is said to be the "Spirit of the Father," and "Spirit of the Son." Galatians 4:6 says, "And because ye are sons, God hath sent forth the Spirit of his Son into your hearts, crying, Abba, Father." Also, "For it is not ye that speak, but the Spirit of your Father which speaketh in you," (Matt. 10:20).

Here are illustrations behind the concept of the *trinity* that have been used throughout the ages. The first one is a more helpful theological chart concerning the ideas we have already covered. The last two are representations of the first chart in concept.

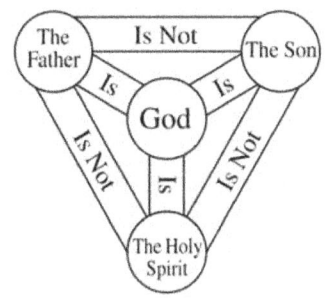  

The Divinity of the Son

"In the beginning was the Word, and the Word was with God, and the Word was God," (John 1:1).

The next two chapters are going to be a little more text and bit less pictures and games. We will still keep our workbook form, but there is a bit of material that we need to go over in order to rightly deal with these doctrines. Also, we would not want to violate the second commandment for the sake of a workbook by strewing its pages with the fictitious ideas of men concerning what they think Jesus looked like or what the Holy Spirit looked like. Those we dispense with knowing they *are* violations of the commands of God.

The person and work of God's Redeemer is one of the largest themes throughout the Bible. From the nature of the work which He was to accomplish, it was necessary that He should be at the same time *both* God and man; One divine person (the Son) in two natures (both divine and human). Since fallen men are those in need of redemption, the Savior must participate in the nature of those whom He came to redeem.

This is an extremely important concept to grasp. Which *one* of the following does *not apply*? (circle only one – there is only one that does not fit). *The Son of God is....*

(a) One divine *person*   (b) one human *nature*   (c) one divine *nature*   (d) one human *person*

Choosing the right answer above determines whether you have fallen in ancient heresy or orthodox biblical truth. It is important that you realize you cannot get this wrong once you learn it. To deny the person or nature of the Son of God in its orthodox form is to deny God. The wrong answer is only "d". Jesus Christ is *not* a human person. He is a divine person (i.e. he is God as a *person* who took on a human *nature*.) Let's understand this more in depth.

Immediately upon the fall of man God instituted the demonstration of His redeeming power through a Redeemer. There are two great truths made clear upon the fall – first, that there is a plurality of persons in the Godhead, and secondly, that one of those persons is especially concerned in the salvation of men to deliver them from all the evils of their apostasy from God's covenant. Genesis 3:15 is often called the *"proto-evangelium"* which literally means "the before Gospel." The Gospel, before it was developed later in Scripture, was stated in Genesis 3:15 this way, "And I will put enmity between thee and the woman, and between thy seed and her seed; it shall bruise thy head, and thou shalt bruise his heel."

The Scriptures in both the Old and New Testament emphasize the need of a Redeemer for men who are steeped in sin and who have broken God's covenant. They are dead, lost, and under the wrath of God, awaiting the final judgment for their sin unless a capable Savior saves them. The Redeemer of the Christian Bible is *God Himself* who takes on the flesh of a human man and dies for the sins of His people. He is the unique God-man, one person with two unmixed but attached natures.

Challenge

Take 30 minutes to locate and write down Scriptures that demonstrate the Messiah is God, but only from the Old Testament.

_____
_____
_____
_____
_____

Old Testament prophecies prove that the Messiah to come was divine. We have a bit of text to work through here so be patient in wading through it. This doctrine is too important to "get wrong." The Suffering Servant of Isaiah 53:1ff is not just a man who dies on a cross.

Rather, the Old Testament prophecies emphatically confirm and prove the divinity of the Messiah *as God*. The *Jewish* Messiah which was to come is *God*. Psalm 2:6-12, where a dialogue takes place between God and His begotten Son, says, "Yet have I set my king upon my holy hill of Zion. I will declare the decree: the LORD hath said unto me, Thou art my Son; this day have I begotten thee. Ask of me, and I shall give thee the heathen for thine inheritance, and the uttermost parts of the earth for thy possession. Thou shalt break them with a rod of iron; thou shalt dash them in pieces like a potter's vessel. Be wise now therefore, O ye kings: be instructed, ye judges of the earth. Serve the LORD with fear, and rejoice with trembling. Kiss the Son, lest he be angry, and ye perish from the way, when his wrath is kindled but a little. Blessed are all they that put their trust in him." Here we see that the Lord begets His Son. This is the eternal begetting of the Son by the Father. Then, the Son is to be worshipped – for the word "Kiss" means "to bow low before." The Son, if not worshipped, will be angry and will cause men to perish in their way.

Psalm 110:1 also attests to the dialogue between God and God. David writes, "The LORD said unto my Lord, Sit thou at my right hand, until I make thine enemies thy footstool." The Messiah will be of the tribe of Judah, David's son, yet David's Lord. The wording here must also be noted. The literal translation says "Yahweh said to my Adonai..." The term "Yahweh" is God's name, literally stated "I am." Each time the designation *Yahweh* is used in the Bible through the Old Testament it refers to the "Great I AM". The title "Adonai" is used in designating God's supreme position as "Lord." So *Yahweh* is speaking to *Adonai*. Here we see God speaking to God. The writer of Hebrews will use this Psalm a number of times to designate the office of the Messiah as the High Priest in the order of Melchizedek.

In Daniel 7:13 we find the title "Son of Man" not as a title of humanity, but of *deity*. "I saw in the night visions, and, behold, one like the Son of man came with the clouds of heaven, and came to the Ancient of days, and they brought him near before him." Two figures are present in this vision, one is the Ancient of Days and one is the Son of Man who rides the clouds of heaven, or the *shekina* glory of heaven. Whoever this Son of Man is, He is *divine*. In fact, He is so brilliant in His glory that it shines about Him as the clouds of heaven. Thick glory clouds of divine brilliance luster before the Ancient of Days as the Son of Man enters the courtroom of God, and the books of judgment are opened. This is Jesus' favorite designation of *Himself* as the Son of Man.

In Micah 5:2 we find the prophecy of the Messiah and His birthplace. But not only does it mark the birthplace of the humanity of the Christ, but it also marks the dual nature that the One to be born is *everlasting*. "But thou, Bethlehem Ephratah, though thou be little among the thousands of Judah, yet out of thee shall he come forth unto me that is to be ruler in Israel; whose goings forth have been from of old, from everlasting." The "goings forth" of the Messiah is "from everlasting." The Messiah is ascribed an incommunicable attribute of God – eternality or the nature of that which is *everlasting*. Only God is everlasting. Yet, we see the Messiah is deemed *everlasting*.

One of the more specific prophecies concerning the Messiah is Isaiah 9:6. Here we read the well-known nativity verse concerning the advent of the Messiah as a child born, and then the designation given to that child. "For unto us a child is born, unto us a son is given: and the government shall be upon his shoulder: and his name shall be called Wonderful, Counsellor, The Mighty God, The everlasting Father, The Prince of Peace." Here the Messiah is called "Wonderful." Why is this? An answer can be found in Judges 13 where we find the narrative of Samson's birth. Manoah and his wife, Samson's parents, encounter the angel of the Lord. After a long conversation concerning the birth of Samson, Manoah asks the angel's name. The response in 13:18 is this, "Why askest thou thus after my name, seeing it is *wonderful*?" The angel's name is wonderful. Usually angels have names like Gabriel or Michael. But this angel has a name too wonderful to mention. After the Angel of the Lord departs, Manoah makes an important statement in Judges 13:22 "We shall surely die for we have seen *God*." This Angel of the Lord, whose name is wonderful, is God. This assists us when considering Isaiah 9:6. The Messiah is God, and His name is Wonderful. However, the prophecy in Isaiah does not stop there. The Messiah is not only called Wonderful, as God, but also called "The Mighty God." If this designation is not explicit enough, the prophecy also deems Him the Everlasting Father. The Messiah is not only the earthly Redeemer, but the Mighty God of the Ages. He is deemed the Everlasting Father, a designation ascribed by Christ to God in the Gospels. The Messiah is designated as God in this prophetic verse of

Isaiah 3 times – once subtly as Wonderful, once explicitly as the Mighty God, and once as the Father.

Along with Isaiah 9:6, as a beloved prophecy concerning the advent of the Messiah, is the prophecy of Immanuel in Isaiah 7:14 which is equally excellent, "Therefore the Lord himself shall give you a sign; Behold, a virgin shall conceive, and bear a son, and shall call his name Immanuel." The Apostle Matthew correctly interprets this in Matthew 1:23 as "God with us." The prophecy concerns the birth narrative of the Christ, as designated and interpreted by a meticulous Jewish accountant (tax collector). Jesus, according to this meticulous tax-collector, is God. The Christ, born of a virgin, is God.

An additional prophecy concerning the Christ, is Jeremiah 23:5-6. "Behold, the days come, saith the LORD, that I will raise unto David a righteous Branch, and a King shall reign and prosper, and shall execute judgment and justice in the earth. In his days Judah shall be saved, and Israel shall dwell safely: and this is his name whereby he shall be called, THE LORD OUR RIGHTEOUSNESS." The raised seed of David will be a righteous Branch. The Messiah shall be from the lineage of David, and will be raised up by God. However, the Messiah will be called, "THE LORD OUR RIGHTEOUSNESS." This designation is a title given to God literally as "Yahweh Tsidkenu." The Messiah is not only raised up by God, but called Yahweh is Righteousness. The Messiah is Yahweh. The Messiah is God.

> "The devil is mighty, I confess it, said Luther, but he will never be Almighty, as my God and Savior is," (*Armilla Catechetica, or a Chain of Theological Principles*).
> John Arrowsmith (1602-1659)

Malachi 3:1 is another important text that speaks of the covenant and messenger of God. "Behold, I will send my messenger, and he shall prepare the way before me: and the Lord, whom ye seek, shall suddenly come to his temple, even the messenger of the covenant, whom ye delight in: behold, he shall come, saith the LORD of hosts." Here we see that the Messiah is identified as "the Lord" who shall come into His temple. He is the messenger of the covenant and the elect Servant in whom God delights. But it is God Himself! Mark 1:2

affirms this in showing that the Malachi verse also attests to the coming of John the Baptist, "it is written in the prophets, Behold, I send my messenger before thy face, which shall prepare thy way before thee." The messenger comes, *then the Lord comes.* Luke also notes this in 1:76, "And thou, child, shalt be called the prophet of the Highest: for thou shalt go before the face of the Lord to prepare his ways." Here Luke records that John will be a prophet to prepare the way of the Highest, who is the Lord to come to His temple. The Messiah is God most High.

Challenge

Take 30 minutes to locate and write down Scriptures that demonstrate the Messiah is God, but only from the New Testament.

_____
_____
_____
_____

The New Testament affirms the Scriptures of the Old Testament that the Messiah is God. Jesus claimed this for Himself, and the Apostles claimed this about Jesus throughout the New Testament. John 1:1-3 states, "In the beginning was the Word, and the Word was with God, and the Word was God. The same was in the beginning with God. All things were made by him; and without him was not anything made that was made." The *Word* in this passage is *Christ*. The Word is God, came from God and created all things. He is the everlasting Logos of God, the very Logic of God himself who came to earth taking on human flesh to save His people.

Further along in the passage of John 1 we find verse 14 stating, "And the Word was made flesh, and dwelt among us, (and we beheld his glory, the glory as of the only begotten of the Father,) full of grace and truth." John not only says that the *Word* is God, but explains that the Word holds the glory of the Father, and is begotten of the Father. The Word came down from heaven, dwelt among men, and His glory, the glory of God alone, shone among men for a time. We know this since this eternal Word was the form of God Himself, as Philippians 2:6-7 explains, "Who, being in the form of God, thought it not robbery to be equal with God: But made himself of no reputation, and took upon him the form of a servant, and was made in the likeness of men." Paul speaks of Jesus Christ here. The Messiah is God, and did not think it robbery to be equal with God. To be equal with God *is to be God*. Only God can be equal with Himself.

In Acts 20:28 we see Luke's record of Christ's work attributed to God Himself, "Take heed therefore unto yourselves, and to all the flock, over the which the Holy Ghost hath made you overseers, to feed the church of God, which he hath purchased with his own blood." The "He" is "God". God purchased the church with His own blood. Jesus Christ dies, and His blood is ascribed *as God's blood*. They are synonymous.

Explain how God (invisible, immutable, *etc.*) has "blood" to a 10 year old.

_____
_____
_____
_____
_____

In the book of Hebrews we find the writer quoting much from the Old Testament to prove the validity of the Messiah's divinity as God. In 1:8-9 the writer says, "But unto the Son he saith, Thy throne, O God, is forever and ever: a sceptre of righteousness is the sceptre of thy kingdom. Thou hast loved righteousness, and hated iniquity; therefore God, even thy God, hath anointed thee with the oil of gladness above thy fellows." He is quoting Psalm 45:7, "Thou lovest righteousness, and hatest wickedness: therefore God, thy God, hath anointed thee with the oil of gladness above thy fellows." Here God is speaking with God. The Anointed One has a throne, and the throne is God's throne. The writer of Hebrews demonstrates that the Messiah is the One, the eternal God Himself, and is greater than the angels and greater than Moses.

 Read Daniel 7:13 and Luke 22:48.

Is "Son of Man" a divine title or a humanistic title for Christ? Does it refer to his divinity or his human nature?

_____

_____

_____

Luke 22:48 speaks about Judas betraying the "Son of Man." Keep in mind, the *divine title* "Son of Man" is used by Christ over 80 times in the Gospels *alone*. This is His favorite designation of Himself. "But Jesus said unto him, Judas, betrayest thou the Son of man with a kiss?" Judas, a man, betrays Jesus, the Son of Man, with a play on worship portrayed as "a kiss". Kissing God, as the Old Testament designates, means worshipping Him. Here, Judas betrays Christ with a kiss. God is betrayed with false worship.

There are a number of New Testament passages that are interpreted in light of Old Testament actions that God has performed, but ascribed to Christ. The tempting of the Lord by the Israelites in the wilderness is recorded numerous times. It is so repetitive that sometimes the reader becomes aggravated at the apparent sin of the Israelites in a given narrative. Some examples of this are the following: Numbers 14:22, "Because all those men which have seen my glory, and my miracles, which I did in Egypt and in the wilderness, and have tempted me now these ten times, and have not hearkened to my voice." Numbers 21:5-6, "And the people spake against God, and against Moses, Wherefore have ye brought us up out of Egypt to die in the wilderness? for there is no bread, neither is there any water; and our soul loatheth this light bread." Also Psalm 95:9 "When your fathers tempted me, proved me, and saw my work..." The Israelites tempted God, and ultimately were bitten by the serpents in the desert as a judgment. We find the New Testament Apostle Paul linking this with Christ in 1 Corinthians 10:9, "Neither let us tempt Christ, as some of them also tempted, and were destroyed of serpents." Paul is saying that we as Christians should not put Christ to the test, or tempt Him. Then he links the temptation of the Israelites to tempting Christ. As we should not tempt Christ now, we ought never follow the Israelites who tempted

Christ then. His phrase "as some of them also tempted" refers back to the fathers, and the Israelites who tempted God. For Paul, to tempt God is to tempt Christ, for they are one and the same.

Another New Testament verse in light of Old Testament prophecies is Heb. 1:10-11, "And, Thou, Lord, in the beginning hast laid the foundation of the earth; and the heavens are the works of thine hands: They shall perish; but thou remainest; and they all shall wax old as doth a garment." This is a description of the Messiah, Jesus Christ. It is a quote from God's works recorded through Psalm 102. In Psalm 102:26 it says, "They shall perish, but thou shalt endure: yea, all of them shall wax old like a garment; as a vesture shalt thou change them, and they shall be changed." Here we see the work of God, again, given as the work of Christ in the New Testament.

In John 12:40-41 the Scriptures say, "He hath blinded their eyes, and hardened their heart; that they should not see with their eyes, nor understand with their heart, and be converted, and I should heal them. These things said Esaias, when he saw his glory, and spake of him", John is quoting Isaiah 6:9-10. Isaiah spoke of Christ, as John interprets this, when the vision came to Isaiah in chapter 6, "And he said, Go, and tell this people, Hear ye indeed, but understand not; and see ye indeed, but perceive not. Make the heart of this people fat, and make their ears heavy, and shut their eyes; lest they see with their eyes, and hear with their ears, and understand with their heart, and convert, and be healed." The One who is holy, holy, holy on the throne is *Christ*, according to John, and the inspired Word. This is the meaning of the vision of Isaiah. The angels in Isaiah's vision say, "holy, holy, holy, is the Lord God Almighty, the whole earth is full of His glory." The Almighty God is Jesus Christ according to John 12:40-41.

In Isaiah 45:23 the text reads, "I have sworn by myself, the word is gone out of my mouth in righteousness, and shall not return, that unto me every knee shall bow, every tongue shall swear." This is mimicked by the Apostle Paul in Romans 14:11, "For it is written, As I live, saith the Lord, every knee shall bow to me, and every tongue shall confess to God." The bowing down is done by men unto the Lord, and the Lord here is Jesus Christ. Paul ascribes the bowing of men to Jesus since the "as I live" and the "unto me" are speaking about God's redemption in Christ.

One of the classic Gospel proclamations is found in Matthew 11:28, "Come unto me, all ye that labor and are heavy laden, and I will give you rest." In this gracious command Jesus says that men should come unto "who?" He says "unto me." This "unto me" is Jesus himself. In Isaiah 45:22 Jesus is borrowing the words of the prophet, "Look unto me, and be ye saved, all the ends of the earth: for I am God, and there is none else." The "unto me" in both passages are parallel. Jesus is affirming His call of the Gospel as God affirms His call in Isaiah. God is the only source of salvation, and Jesus borrows this to show that He is the only source of salvation – Jesus is God.

Find two passages in the Gospels that Jesus says directly or indirectly that he is God.

_____
_____
_____
_____

Paul also makes this affirmative in Ephesians 4:8-9, "Wherefore he saith, When he ascended up on high, he led captivity captive, and gave gifts unto men." Here he quotes Psalm 68:18, "Thou hast ascended on high, thou hast led captivity captive: thou hast received gifts for men; yea, for the rebellious also, that the LORD God might dwell among them." The Psalmist is speaking of God's works; literally "Yahweh Elohim." Paul then takes this designation and interprets this as Christ's work in His ascension to heaven. In Christ's work of redemption, He gives gifts to men and leads captivity (those dead in sin) captive (now free in Christ). The work of God, again, is attributed to Christ.

In 1 John 5:20 Jesus is called the true God, and eternal life itself, "And we know that the Son of God is come, and hath given us an understanding, that we may know him that is true, and we are in him that is true, even in his Son Jesus Christ." This is the true God, and eternal life. Paul affirms this in Romans 9:5 where he called Jesus Christ, "God blessed forever." "Whose are the fathers, and of whom as concerning the flesh Christ came, who is over all, God blessed forever. Amen." Jesus is the eternally blessed God. In Titus 2:13, Paul called Jesus, "the Great God and Savior." He says, "Looking for that blessed hope, and the glorious appearing of the great God and our Saviour Jesus Christ." Jesus is the Great God and He is the Savior. In John 20:28 Thomas gives a two-fold confession, "And Thomas answered and said unto him, My Lord and my God." Not only is Christ Lord, but He is also God.

Did the Pharisees understand that Jesus spoke about himself as GOD? (Circle) YES NO

In John 8:58-59, we find a raging discourse between the Pharisees and Jesus. This debate builds up into hatred of Christ on the part of the Jews. The text says, "Jesus said unto them, Verily, verily, I say unto you, Before Abraham was, I am. Then took they up stones to cast at him: but Jesus hid himself, and went out of the temple, going through the midst of them, and so passed by." Why did they pick up stones to stone Him? Because they knew exactly what was being said. Jesus was claiming to be the deliverer of the Israelites from Egypt. He was the, "I Am" who talked with Moses in Exodus 4 at the burning bush. This is enhanced when we remember His previous discussion with them in John 5:17-19, "But Jesus answered them, My Father worketh hitherto, and I work. Therefore the Jews sought the more to kill him, because he not only had broken the Sabbath, but said also that God was his Father, making himself equal with God. Then answered Jesus and said unto them, Verily, verily, I say unto you, The Son can do nothing of himself, but what he seeth the Father do: for what things soever he doeth, these also doeth the Son likewise." Jesus does what the Father does. Jesus can do this because *He is God*. He is on equal terms with the Father, and is able to accomplish the same acts as the Father. The Jews understood exactly what he was saying and desired to kill Him. Then came the incident when He blatantly stated He was the, "I AM" or Yahweh Himself. With this statement the Jews desired to stone Him. Jesus claimed to be God, and said He was Yahweh Himself.

Find a passage in the New Testament that correlates to the attribute listed below for each of them as they apply to Jesus. I've done the first one for you...(look those up and read them).

OMNISCIENT: JOHN 1:48, JOHN 21:17 _____

ETERNAL: _____

ALL-POWERFUL: _____

OMNIPRESENT: _____

GLORIOUS: _____

IMMUNTABLE: _____

God is glorious. He alone is most glorious and has a glory only known to Him. It is part of Him. He does not share it with others. But Jesus, in John 17:5 says, "And now, O Father, glorify thou me with thine own self with the glory which I had with thee before the world was." Jesus had a divine glory before the world even existed. The only way such a glory could be ascribed to Christ is if he was God.

In John 1:1 Jesus is ascribed attributes of *eternity*. "In the beginning was the Word, and the Word was with God, and the Word was God. The same was in the beginning with God. All things were made by him; and without him was not anything made that was made." He is the Word which is with God from the beginning. That means He is everlasting. He is also the Creator and has the power to create out of nothing. His creative ability proves His Omnipotence. His attributes are the same as God's attributes because He is God.

Jesus is ascribed attributes of *omnipresence* as in Matthew 18:20, "For where two or three are gathered together in my name, there am I in the midst of them." This does not mean that the humanity of Christ is everywhere present, for He would not be really human. His humanity would be swallowed up somehow in the divinity. Or His divinity would be negated if mixed with the humanity. In either case, to attribute a mixing of the natures is to fall into unorthodox heresy. Rather, His divine nature, as God, is everywhere present. He is able to be in the midst of His people wherever two or three are gathered for such purposes. Jesus says "I," proving that He believed He was able to be anywhere in the world at the same time with the two or three gathered together. How could He be in the midst of so many churches on a given day if He was not God?

Not only is Christ omnipresent, but another theological designation may be ascribed to Him called "immensity." In John 3:13 it says, "And no man hath ascended up to heaven, but he that came down from heaven, even the Son of man which is in heaven." This is such a rich verse. Jesus is not only the one who came down from heaven, but in His divinity, He is still in heaven. The phrase "which is in heaven" demonstrates the immensity of the divine being. Not only is the divine Son in the human nature of Christ walking the earth at that time, but the divine Son continually fills heaven as the immense God of the Ages.

Since Jesus Christ is God He must, necessarily, be *all-powerful*. Both Revelation 1:8 and 11:17 show us that Jesus is ascribed attributes of omnipotence. "I am he that liveth, and was dead; and, behold, I am alive forevermore, Amen; and have the keys of hell and of death," and also, "Saying, We give thee thanks, O Lord God Almighty, which art, and wast, and art to come; because thou hast taken to thee thy great power, and hast reigned." Jesus has the keys of death and hell, which means He is all-powerful over death. He is the sovereign Lord over hell and death. The only one who could have this power is God. God is the All-Powerful Sovereign who controls hell and death. Jesus can raise Himself from the dead, and He is in command of those who are dead and in hell as Lord God Almighty.

In John 5:17, Jesus is also ascribed attributes as the Father. "But Jesus answered them, My Father worketh hitherto, and I work." Jesus works in the same manner as the Father. Again, if He was working the works of the Father, or making Himself equal to accomplishing the same works of the Father, He must be God to accomplish these works. His work is the same quality as the Father's. The Jews hated these sayings because they knew he was making Himself equal with God.

The Gospels also record that Jesus was omniscient. The Son of God communicated the knowledge that the divine nature possessed to the human nature in certain instances; not completely, but in varied amounts. This could only be accomplished if Jesus was God. And it is not that the writers thought He knew some things, but all things, which is only something

God could do. We see this in John 1:48, "Nathaniel saith unto him, Whence knowest thou me? Jesus answered and said unto him, Before that Philip called thee, when thou wast under the fig tree, I saw thee." Peter says to Him in John 21:17, "Thou knowest all things." Jesus knew specific details that only God could know. For instance, in Revelation 2:3 we find Him saying, "And hast borne, and hast patience, and for my name's sake hast labored, and hast not fainted. Nevertheless I have somewhat against thee, because thou hast left thy first love." How could Jesus know all these works about the church at Ephesus? He has to be omniscient to be a searcher of the heart to know their patience, labor, and endurance – not to mention their dispositions concerning their love for Him. Jesus knows all things because He is God.

The writer of Hebrews also makes note that Jesus, the Son, is immutable – He does not change. Hebrews 1:11-12 say, "They shall perish; but thou remainest; and they all shall wax old as doth a garment; and as a vesture shalt thou fold them up, and they shall be changed: but thou art the same, and thy years shall not fail." He is the same, and His years never fail. He remains forever. Jesus is able to remain the same forever because He is God. This does not mean He does not age, or does not grow in His human nature. Rather, it does mean that Christ, as the divine Son of God, in His divinity, never changes.

Not only is Jesus God, but Paul describes His unique makeup as the One who holds the fullness of the Godhead *bodily*. Colossians 2:9 teaches us this, "For in him dwelleth all the fullness of the Godhead bodily." If you desire to see God, then look to Christ. He is the image of the Divine Godhead, and that image, that perfection, is manifest only in Him since He is God. No man could ever claim this – and no man except Jesus Christ has ever done so. Christ claimed these, backed up those claims, and is ascribed them repeatedly by the writers of the New Testament.

As God, Jesus Christ backs up the claim and acts like God – He is the Creator. Colossians 1:16-17 says, "For by him were all things created, that are in heaven, and that are in earth, visible and invisible, whether they be thrones, or dominions, or principalities, or powers: all things were created by him, and for him: And he is before all things, and by him all things consist." This is a very rich text. He creates all things, no matter what they are, even principalities and powers (which may refer to angelic beings). They were created by Him, but also for Him. They are to give Him all the glory, praise and honor His name deserves. But Paul does not stop there – he says all things consist as a result of His sustaining power. The earth, the heavens, the universe itself, would fall apart if Christ did not uphold it by the power of His omnipotent will. All things consist through Him, for Him, and by Him.

Jesus is also the One who elects men to salvation. In John 13:18 He elects the apostles, and damns the betrayer, Judas, "I speak not of you all: I know whom I have chosen: but that the scripture may be fulfilled, He that eateth bread with me hath lifted up his heel against me." Judas was not chosen, and thus is deemed the one who lifts his heel against the Anointed.

In 1 Timothy 6:15 Jesus is called Lord of Lords, "Which in his times he shall shew, who is the blessed and only Potentate, the King of kings, and Lord of lords; Who only hath immortality, dwelling in the light which no man can approach unto; whom no man hath seen, nor can see: to whom be honor and power everlasting. Amen." He is the Potentate, which means He is the all-powerful one. He is the One who holds immortality, and dwells in a pure, unapproachable light. Only God can live in unapproachable light. This is ascribed to Christ. Jesus is the everlasting God who lives in unapproachable light as God.

Jesus has the power to reveal or hide salvation from men. This argues His divinity since all through the Old Testament God is the only one who can save or damn. Matthew 11:26-27 says, "Even so, Father: for so it seemed good in thy sight. All things are delivered unto me of my Father: and no man knoweth the Son, but the Father; neither knoweth any man the Father, save the Son, and he to whomsoever the Son will reveal him." If Christ desires to reveal salvation He shall do so, and if He wishes to hide it from other men He may do so. The reason He is able to declare or hide salvation is because He is God. He has the right to give eternal life as He sees fit as in John 5:21b, "For as the Father raiseth up the dead, and quickeneth them; even so the Son quickeneth whom he will." He does not do this to all. He only quickens the elect.

Find two passages in the Gospels that Jesus is worshipped.

_____
_____
_____
_____
_____

Since Christ is omniscient, He answers the prayers of the saints, and only God is able to do this. John 14:13 "And whatsoever ye shall ask in my name, that will I do, that the Father may be glorified in the Son," (cf. 2 Cor. 12:8-9). How could a finite man possibly know all the prayers of the disciples if they prayed in various places and at sundry times? It is impossible unless Jesus is God.

Not only does He disclose salvation to men, and answer prayer, but he also forgives sin. Only God is able to forgive sins. The passage in Matthew 9:6, Mark 2:10, and Luke 5:24 bears this out – He forgives sins and only God can do this. "But that ye may know that the Son of man hath power on earth to forgive sins, (then saith he to the sick of the palsy,) Arise, take up thy bed, and go unto thine house." Here the Jews wondered who this man was who said He could forgive sins. So Jesus asks them which is easier, to forgive sins, or cause the man with palsy to rise up and walk. To demonstrate His divinity He accomplishes both, for both are impossible with men but possible with God.

> "The safest course is to place our whole trust and confidence in the mercy of God and merits of Christ for eternal salvation," (*Stand Still*).
> John Brinsley (1600-1665)

Why do you think Brinsley makes a distinction between "the mercy of God" and the merits of Christ" that concern eternal salvation? Are these *actually* different? or not?

_____
_____
_____

Throughout the Old Testament God prods men to look to Him to be saved, and put their trust in Him. He has stretched His hand out to a rebellious people all day long. There are those who took up the gift of faith and believed God. Abraham was justified by faith, through his belief in the promises of God. However, in the New Testament *Jesus is the object of faith*. In John 14:1 He says, "Let not your heart be troubled: ye believe in God, believe also in me." Jesus sets Himself as equal with God. The same belief that people have in God should also be given to Him. Believing in God is believing in Christ *because they are the same*.

Christ's power is so extensive and awesome that He can *call men out of the grave*. John 5:28-29 says, "Marvel not at this: for the hour is coming, in the which all that are in the graves shall hear his voice, And shall come forth; they that have done good, unto the resurrection of life; and they that have done evil, unto the resurrection of damnation." Jesus has such power over death that the sound of His voice can summon the decayed corpses from the ground to hearken unto His command. And His power in the last day is recorded as so great, that His return shall be a day unlike any other. Matthew 24:20 says, "But pray ye that your flight be not in the winter, neither on the sabbath day: For then shall be great tribulation, such as was not since the beginning of the world to this time, no, nor ever shall be." He will return in power and great glory. The sun, moon and stars will fall from the sky and His glory will outshine their brilliance. His glory will be so radiant that the shining of the sun would seem dim.

Worship is also ascribed to God and Jesus Christ. In Exodus 20:1ff the text reads, "And God spake all these words, saying, I am the LORD thy God, which have brought thee out of the land of Egypt, out of the house of bondage. Thou shalt have no other gods before me. Thou shalt not make unto thee any graven image, or any likeness of any thing that is in heaven above, or that is in the earth beneath, or that is in the water under the earth: Thou shalt not bow down thyself to them, nor serve them: for I the LORD thy God am a jealous God, visiting the iniquity of the fathers upon the children unto the third and fourth generation of them that hate me; And shewing mercy unto thousands of them that love me, and keep my commandments. Thou shalt not take the name of the LORD thy God in vain; for the LORD will not hold him guiltless that taketh his name in vain." Here we find the object, means and manner of worship. God alone is to be worshipped and no other gods should be tolerated. To worship other gods is to excite the anger of God upon the rebellious sinner. God is emphatic and explicit that no other gods are to be worshipped because He is the One True Living God of the Ages. All the other gods are but dumb idols. In Deuteronomy 6:13-16 Moses says, "Thou shalt fear the LORD thy God, and serve him, and shalt swear by his name. Ye shall not go after other gods, of the gods of the people which are round about you; (For the LORD thy God is a jealous God among you) lest the anger of the LORD thy God be kindled against thee, and destroy thee from off the face of the earth. Ye shall not tempt the LORD your God, as ye tempted him in Massah." God is angered when His people are led astray to worship false gods. His anger is kindled like a fire. Judges 2:12 says, "And they forsook the LORD God of their fathers, which brought them out of the land of Egypt, and followed other gods, of the gods of the people that were round about them, and bowed themselves unto them, and provoked the LORD to anger." When this happens the Lord enacts judgment for the sin of His people. Jeremiah 1:16 and 7:18 declares, "And I will utter my judgments against them touching all their wickedness, who have forsaken me, and have burned incense unto other gods, and worshipped the works of their own hands...The children gather wood, and the fathers kindle the fire, and the women knead their dough, to make cakes to the queen of heaven, and to pour out drink offerings unto other gods, that they may provoke me to anger." God's people are to shun the foreign gods of the pagans as in Daniel 3:18, "But if not, be it known unto thee, O king, that we will not serve thy gods, nor worship the golden image which thou hast set up." And even Paul remarks that there is only one true God in 1 Corinthians 8:5, "For though there be that are called gods, whether in heaven or in earth, (as there be gods many, and lords many,) But to us there is but one God, the Father, of whom are all things, and we in him; and one Lord Jesus Christ, by whom are all things, and we by him." All this is said to show that God alone is to be worshipped. To worship any other but the True and Living God is to break the Law of the Lord and to disobey Him with heinous sin and rebellion.

If God will not share *his glory* with anyone else, and Jesus *retains such glory* as the glorious Savior, what does that tell you about all the Old Testament passages concerning the glory of God?

_____
_____
_____
_____
_____

It is also important to remember that God will not share the glory He has or is exalted in with another. Isaiah 42:8 asserts, "I am the LORD: that is my name: and my glory will I not give to another, neither my praise to graven images." God requires that men worship only the true God, and no others. However, Jesus is often worshipped through the New Testament, and even the Old Testament by way of prophecy. This is a remarkable fact for two reasons, 1) Jesus allowed Himself to be worshipped, which means, He was God and *knew* this, and 2) Only God is to be worshipped as the hundreds of Scriptural passages on the subject prove. He shares in the glory of the Lord. God shares His glory with Him. If Jesus was not God, then on this one point alone the entire Christian faith falls and turns to rubble.

Jesus tells the disciples that they should believe in God as their object of faith. But in John 14:1, as said earlier, Jesus says, "Let not your heart be troubled: ye believe in God, believe also in me." Belief in God is an act of worship and trust in His name. Jesus says that we should believe in Him as we believe in God. The element of faith is the same. In this trust, Jesus is magnified. The Old Testament prophecy concerning the Son in Psalm 2:12, is helpful in this, "Kiss the Son, lest he be angry, and ye perish from the way, when his wrath is kindled but a little. Blessed are all they that put their trust in him." Those who trust the Son are called blessed. He is to be kissed. The Son is to be worshipped and trusted because He is God.

Jesus Christ is also to be honored in the same way as the Father as John 5:22 demonstrates, "That all men should honor the Son, even as they honor the Father. He that honoureth not the Son honoureth not the Father which hath sent him." Both are equally honored, and this could not be done unless Christ was God. Otherwise, we would be honoring a mere man instead of that which is due unto *God alone*.

Not only do men worship Jesus, but angels are commanded to worship Him as well. Hebrews 1:6 speaks of Christ when it says, "And again, when he bringeth in the firstbegotten into the world, he saith, And let all the angels of God worship him." In fact, angels, men, and all creatures are commanded to bow down to Him and worship Him, "all shall bow to Him. Wherefore God also hath highly exalted him, and given him a name which is above every name: That at the name of Jesus every knee should bow, of things in heaven, and things in earth, and things under the earth; And that every tongue should confess that Jesus Christ is Lord, to the glory of God the Father." (Philippians 2:9-11) This is also seen in Revelation 5:13, "And every creature which is in heaven, and on the earth, and under the earth, and such as are in the sea, and all that are in them, heard I saying, Blessing, and honor, and glory, and power, be unto him that sitteth upon the throne, and unto the Lamb forever and ever." The Lamb, Jesus Christ, is worshipped forever and ever because he is God.

He was worshipped often: a leper worshipped Him in Mathew 8:2, "And, behold, there came a leper and worshipped him, saying, Lord, if thou wilt, thou canst make me clean." A ruler worshipped Him in Matthew 9:18, "While he spake these things unto them, behold, there came a certain ruler, and worshipped him, saying, My daughter is even now dead: but come and lay thy hand upon her, and she shall live." The disciples worshipped Him in Matthew 14:33, "Then they that were in the ship came and worshipped him, saying, of a truth thou art the Son of God." A Canaanite woman worshipped Him in Matthew 15:25, "Then came she and worshipped him, saying, Lord, help me." In Matthew 28:9, 17, after the resurrection, the disciples worshipped Him again, "And as they went to tell his disciples, behold, Jesus met them, saying, All hail. And they came and held him by the feet, and worshipped him. And when they saw him, they worshipped him: but some doubted." (The idea that some doubted is utterly amazing!) Demons worshipped Him as with the Gadarene Demoniac, "But when he saw Jesus afar off, he ran and worshipped him." (Mark 5:6) On the road to Emmaus the two disciples worshipped Him in Luke 24:52, "And they worshipped him, and returned to Jerusalem with great joy." Even a poor blind man who was healed, worshipped Him, "And he said, Lord, I believe. And he worshipped him." (John 9:38)

Jesus *allowed* men to worship Him, and *elicited* that worship. This is something an Israelite would have been stoned for, and the Jews certainly desire to stone Jesus as a result. Demons, angels, lepers, Gentiles, Jews, his own disciples, and so on, worshiped Him. Over and over we see that Jesus Christ was worshipped, and those who worshipped Him acted accordingly – He deserved to be worshipped because He is God.

What does it mean that the Son of God pre-existed? Does this apply to his human nature or his divine nature or both?

_____
_____
_____
_____

Lastly, the pre-existence of the Son must be noted. In John 3:13 we find that the Son ascends and descends from heaven, "And no man hath ascended up to heaven, but he that came down from heaven, even the Son of man which is in heaven." As with His immensity, we see that His origin is "from heaven" and that He "came down" from heaven. His origins are not of the earth, but of heaven. This is reiterated in John 6:38, "For I came down from heaven, not to do mine own will, but the will of him that sent me." If this was not true, Jesus Christ would have said he was born of Mary and Joseph to do the will of the Father.

He also attests that no one except for Him has seen the Father, "Not that any man hath seen the Father, save he which is of God, he hath seen the Father." (John 6:46) This means that Jesus Christ was aware of His divine nature as present with the Father before time was created. Only He has seen the Father. And His residence with the Father is spoken of in John 6:62. Here Jesus will ascend to heaven where he had been before, "What, and if ye shall see the Son of man ascend up where he was before?" Then if these words are not clear enough, the eternal Logos of John's Gospel says this, "And he said unto them, Ye are from beneath; I am from above: ye are of this world; I am not of this world." (John 8:23) If this statement was false, the entire Christian religion and all Christians from the time of Christ until now, have been partakers of a farce. They would show themselves as the most stupid and ignorant people of all time. Rather, the disciples did not run from this statement because they knew the truth of the claim. Not only had Christ proven it, but also, they had seen His divinity in the transfiguration.

His claims lay with the eternal residence of the Father as stated in John 8:42, "Jesus said unto them, If God were your Father, ye would love me: for I proceeded forth and came from God; neither came I of myself, but he sent me." He has close relations with the Father which again proves His divinity from everlasting, "He has seen the Father, "I speak that which I have seen with my Father: and ye do that which ye have seen with your father." (John 8:38) And also John 16:28, "I came forth from the Father, and am come into the world: again, I leave the world, and go to the Father." If the Father is God and Jesus came out from the Father and shall return to His unique relationship with Him, this argues His eternal preexistence as the Son of God. Otherwise, the Father is not divine if Jesus Christ is not divine, for they are one.

The student of Scripture cannot doubt the claims of the prophecies concerning Christ, the writers of the Bible and their attestation of Christ, the recorded claims of those opposed to Christ (who wanted to kill Him for His claims), those who worshipped Christ, and the claims of Christ Himself. Whether a person believes in Jesus Christ or not is not the issue here. The issue is that the prophecies of the Bible, the disciples, the hearers, the followers, the gainsayers and the words of Christ all point to the undeniable fact that these witnesses *knew Christ was God.* They either hated Him for it, or worshipped Him as a result of it. Jesus Christ knew He was God. He attested to it through His words, actions, and witness of the truth. No one can simply call Christ a good teacher. That is the voice and opinion of the non-thinker. Jesus Christ cannot just be a good teacher or a moral man. That is not in the equation at all. There are only two choices: He is either Lord of heaven and earth, the Righteous Judge of the World, *or* He is a lunatic and madman, a deceiver worse than the devil.

If someone simply reads the Bible with a cursory reading, should they come away with knowing Jesus is God? How?

___

THE SAVIOR, JESUS CHRIST, IN HIS PERSON AND WORK

The Bible teaches that Jesus Christ is truly man, *i.e.*, He had a perfect or complete *human nature*. The Bible also teaches He was truly God, or had a perfect *divine nature* (as we have seen in the previous *section*). The Bible shows us that there is no confusion with these two natures and one person. The same *person* who said, "I thirst," humanly speaking, said, "Before Abraham was, I AM," speaking as the eternal God. This is the entire doctrine of the incarnation as it lies in the Scriptures and in the faith of the Church.

TRULY MAN

The Bible teaches that Christ is truly man, or has a complete human nature. He had a *true* body and a *rational* soul. By a true body is meant a material body, composed of flesh and blood, in everything essential like the bodies of ordinary men.

Read Hebrews 2:14, Luke 24:39, and Mark 14:34.

What constitutes a perfect or complete human nature based on these Scriptures? Did Jesus have a perfect or complete human nature?

___

CHRIST IS TRULY GOD

The Bible teaches that Christ was *truly* God. He is called God, the mighty God, the great God, God over all, Jehovah, Lord, the Lord of lords and the King of kings. As discussed earlier, all divine attributes are ascribed to Him. He is declared to be omnipresent, omniscient, almighty, and immutable, the same yesterday, today, and forever. He is the creator, governor and ruler of the universe. He is the object of worship to all creatures, the object of reverence, love, faith, and devotion. As Supreme Judge, men and angels are responsible to Him for their character and conduct. He declares that He and the Father are one; that those who had seen Him had seen the Father also. "I and my Father are one," (John 10:30). *Jesus is God.*

CHRIST IS ONE PERSON

Thirdly, though He is perfect man and perfect God, He is only *one person;* one person with two natures. For example, the Son of God never addresses the Son of Man as a different person from Himself. They are the same person. The Scriptures reveal *one* Christ. He always says *I, me, mine.* He is always addressed as *Thou, thee, thine.* He is always spoken of as *He, his, him.* It was the same person to whom it was said, "Thou art not yet fifty years old;" and "Thou, Lord, in the beginning hast laid the foundation of the earth, and the heavens are the works of thine hands."

"And, firstly, it seems to me, that He was pleased (as is said in the Epistle to the Hebrews) to communicate with us, in flesh and blood, by the benefit of His Incarnation," (*Letters to Calvin*).

Peter Marytr Vermigli (1499-1562)

Based on what we have studied so far, explain why you believe Jesus needed to come and communicate with us in flesh and blood?

_____
_____
_____
_____
_____

The individual personality of Christ is taught in the Bible as clearly as that of any other *person* of whose history the Scriptures give record. In teaching that Christ had a perfect human and a perfect divine nature, and is one person, the Bible teaches the whole doctrine of the incarnation. The union of two natures to one person is called the *Hypostatical Union*. The elements united are the divine and human nature. In this connection is meant *substance* which is where the word *hypostasis* comes from. These two natures are united but not mingled or confounded. There is no transfer of the attributes of one nature to the other. It is not a mere indwelling of the divine nature or a moral or sympathetic union, nor a temporary and mutable relation between the two. They render Christ the God-man without any incompatibility. [For a full treatment of heretical doctrines concerning the person and work of Christ see my work, *Historical Theology Made Easy*.]

[
"Justification is God's action where he pardons all sins and imputes righteousness to every true believer by grace on the merit of Jesus," (*The Way to Heaven*).

John Philips (1585-1663)
]

JESUS CHRIST THE MEDIATOR

The name of Christ is the only name whereby men can be saved. Acts 4:12, "Neither is there salvation in any other: for there is none other name under heaven given among men, whereby we must be saved," (Acts 4:12). The design of the incarnation of the Son of God was to reconcile His people to God, and reconciliation occurs through the work and merit of the Mediator.

Define *merit*.

_____
_____
_____
_____

To be a Mediator between God and men, Jesus Christ must be God and He must be man. The Mediator between God and man must be sinless; "holy, harmless, undefiled, and separate from sinners," (Hebrews 7:26). Christ was without sin (Hebrews 4:15; 1 Peter 2:22). These qualifications are essential, of which, Christ fulfilled them all. It was *necessary* that Christ should be *both* God and man in two distinct natures and one person, in order to affect our redemption.

In His mediatorial work Christ was our Prophet, Priest and King – the threefold designation of His work on our behalf. As *prophet* He is one who speaks for another. "The word which ye hear is not mine, but the Father's which sent me," (John 14:24). As a *priest* He offers up the proper sacrifice to redeem His people in the order of a High Priest. "Thou art a priest forever after the order of Melchizedec," (Psalm 110:4). He *expiates* our guilt and makes *propitiation* for us before God as a vicarious sacrifice, and continually stands as the infinite sacrifice of God interceding on behalf of His people. *Vicarious* suffering is suffering endured by one person in the stead of another. Expiation and propitiation mean that Christ took away the guilt of the sinner (*expiates*) that He dies for (that it actually occurs upon the cross by His death), and then satisfies the justice of God (*propitiation*).

"The Lord Jesus, by his perfect obedience and sacrifice of Himself, which He through the eternal Spirit once offered up unto God, hath fully satisfied the justice of his Father; and purchased not only reconciliation, but an everlasting inheritance in the kingdom of heaven for all those whom the Father hath given unto Him," (*The 1647 Westminster Confession* 8:5).

"As *king* He rules and reigns over His Church and the world, "Rejoice greatly, O daughter of Zion, shout, O daughter of Jerusalem; Behold, thy King cometh unto thee; he is just, and having salvation; lowly, and riding upon an ass, and upon a colt the foal of an ass," (Zech. 9:9). And, "These shall make war with the Lamb, and the Lamb shall overcome them: for he is Lord of lords, and King of kings: and they that are with him are called, and chosen, and faithful," (Rev. 17:14).

This work of the Mediator satisfied the demands of God's Law perfectly. A sinless, infinite sacrifice was given and accepted *by God*. As a result, this one sacrifice has perfected forever them that are sanctified, (Hebrews 10:14). No other is needed, and no other is possible. Those who reject God's method of salvation *perish*. To them there, "remaineth no more sacrifice for sins," (Hebrews 10:26).

EXTENT OF THE ATONEMENT OF CHRIST

The Bible teaches that since expiation and propitiation occur *at the time* of the sacrifice of Christ, then those for whom He died are actually saved and cannot but be saved. As a result, those for whom Christ died are actually, truly and eternally saved by *His* work. God, from all eternity, elected some to everlasting life, and had a special reference to their salvation in the mission and work of His Son. This limits the *extent* of the atonement, not the *power* or *worth* of the atonement.

> "Christ died either for all of the sins of all men; some of the sins of all men or all the sins of some men," (*Death of Death in the Death of Christ*).
> John Owen (1616-1683)

Which one is right? (Circle it.) *Christ died either for:*

1. All of the sins of all men.
2. Some of the sins of all men.
3. All the sins of some men.

Break it down: Christ died either for all of the sins of all men (thus all men *are saved*); some of the sins of all men (Roman Catholic's view which entails a *further work* by the sinner to be saved) or all the sins of some men (which is the Gospel, and the biblical teaching that Christ secures the salvation of those men at the time of His death). There are no other views to take. Christ's death doesn't create a "way" for men to work for salvation (*Arminianism*), nor does Christ save all men (*Universalism*). Rather, like the paschal lamb of the Old Testament that was given on behalf of God's covenant people, Christ is given on behalf of *His sheep* – not the goats.

Passages demonstrating that Christ's saving power actually occurs and saves are too numerous to cite exhaustively.

Match the phrase to the Scripture.

Christ gave Himself for His church.	John 15:13
Christ laid down his life for His sheep.	John 10:15
Christ laid down his life for His friends.	John 11:52
Christ died to gather the children of God.	Acts 10:28
Christ purchased the Church.	Ephesians 5:25

God from eternity gave a people to His Son. The infinite love of God to His people is the biblical motive for the gift of His Son. Their salvation is the design of His mission. As their representative Head and substitution, He came into the world, assumed a human nature, fulfilled all righteousness, and bore the curse of the Law. So, the salvation of all those given to Him by the Father is rendered *absolutely certain*. In a desperate world, where sin is seen everywhere, the hope of this Gospel renders sure the work of the Mediator for all *those that have an interest* in God and His Son Jesus Christ.

HUMILIATION AND EXALTATION

What does it mean to be humiliated, and how does this apply to Christ?

_____
_____
_____
_____
_____

The humiliation of Christ includes His incarnation, humanity and death. His exaltation includes His rising from the dead, ascension and current reigning in heaven.

In His humiliation He was born of a woman and made under the Law (Gal. 4:4). He partook of humanity in taking on flesh and blood, (Heb. 2:14). The Apostle Paul says that He made himself, "of no reputation in becoming man," (Phil. 2:7). He was made under the Law. "I came down from heaven, not to do mine own will, but the will of him that sent me," (John 6:38). Hebrews says, "Though he were a Son, yet learned he obedience," (Heb. 5:8). He suffered and died on a cross. "Being found in fashion as a man, he humbled himself, and became obedient unto death, even the death of the cross," (Phil. 2:8). All this was for God's glory and our salvation. His subjection to the Law and to the will of the Father was voluntary and vicarious for us and for our salvation. Scripture teaches that He was, "made sin" (2 Cor. 5:21), or, *treated as a sinner*, "numbered with the transgressors" (Isa. 53:12).

What does it mean that Christ was exalted?
_____
_____
_____
_____
_____

In His exaltation Christ was resurrected, ascended to heaven, sits at the right hand of God and will come to judge the world at the last day. A fundamental truth of the gospel is that Christ is risen, "If Christ be not risen then is our preaching vain, and your faith is also vain," (1 Cor. 15:14). The next step in the exaltation of Christ was His ascension to heaven. Mark 16:19 says, after Jesus had spoken to His disciples, "He was received up into heaven." After His final words to the disciples in Acts 1:9-11, Scripture records, "When he had spoken these things, while they beheld, he was taken up; and a cloud received him out of their sight. And while they looked steadfastly toward heaven, as he went up, behold two men stood by them in white apparel; which also said, Ye men of Galilee, why stand ye gazing up into heaven? This same Jesus, which is taken up from you into heaven, shall so come in like manner as ye have seen him go into heaven." After His ascension Christ is now sitting at the right hand of God. Christ, "sat down on the right hand of the Majesty on high," (Heb. 1:3). Ephesians 1:20-22 states, that God raised Christ from the dead, "and set him at his own right hand in the heavenly places, far above all principality, and power, and might, and dominion, and every name that is named, not only in this world, but also in that which is to come; and hath put all things under his feet." Finally, Christ is coming to judge the world. This is the last step in His exaltation. Acts 17:31 states, "Because he hath appointed a day, in which he will judge the world in righteousness by that man whom he hath ordained; whereof he hath given assurance unto all men, in that he hath raised him from the dead."

"Necessary, not absolutely, but by divine decree, that the Mediator should be God, and become man. Neither man nor angel, though pure, could have sufficed. The Son of God behoved to come down. Man in innocence could not penetrate to God without a Mediator, much less could he after the fall," (*Institutes of the Christian Religion*).

John Calvin (1509-1564)

The Divinity of the Holy Spirit

"The grace of the Lord Jesus Christ, and the love of God, and the communion of the Holy Ghost, be with you all. Amen," (2 Cor. 13:14).

> "Love indeed proceeds from faith and hope, as the Holy Spirit proceeds from both the other persons of the Trinity," (*The Saints Will Judge the World*).
> Daniel Cawdrey (1588-1664)

How would you explain the procession of the Holy Spirit from the Father and the Son to a 10 year old?

_____
_____
_____
_____
_____

Scripture is permeated with truths identifying and explaining the person and work of the Holy Spirit in creation, through the Messiah, and in the work among believers. Historically and exegetically, truths about this doctrine are classified within the larger framework of the *Trinity*. Truths surrounding the Trinity and the person of the Holy Spirit are directly related, as we have already discussed.

There is one God or divine essence. The same numerical divine essence is common to three divine Persons known as the Father, Son and Holy Spirit. Between these three persons of the Godhead, there exists a natural order of subsistence and operation. This operation teaches that the first Person has life in Himself (John 5:26) and that the second and third Persons subsist and act from the first. This order of Persons is from *eternity*. Their order of subsistence is the ground and reason there are three names or designations of the Godhead – Father, Son and Holy Spirit. But *who* is this Spirit?

> "Sin against the Holy Spirit is against the entire authority, love and work of God and the work of all three divine Persons in our salvation," (*The Marks of a Godly Man*).
>
> Daniel Burgess (1645-1713)

Read the quote above. Why do you think *Burgess* thinks this?

_____
_____
_____
_____
_____

Read Genesis 1:2, Job 26:13, and Job 33:4.

How is the Spirit of God introduced in the Bible? What is ascribed to him right out of the gate?

_____
_____
_____
_____
_____

In the Old Testament the Spirit of God is first introduced as the Creator of all things. Man, one being among all things, is also created and filled with the breath of life, or a special operation of the Spirit imparting His image upon man. Adam attained originally what Christ would later replenish in some fallen men – the *gift* of the Spirit. As a result of the fall of man, the Spirit withdrew from him and he was then designated as "flesh" (Gen. 4:3). The image of God that Adam was first created in was wholly corrupted and defiled by his sin in the garden under the temptation of the devil (Gen. 3:1-15; John 3:6). Since the fall, the plan of salvation has encompassed the replenishment of the defiled image of God by the operation of the Spirit upon wicked men who receive mercy through mediation.

Was Abraham, the father of our faith, indwelt by the Spirit of God? Can anyone go to heaven without being indwelt and saved by the Spirit of God? Is Abraham in heaven?

_____
_____
_____
_____

Throughout the Old Testament the Spirit worked upon and in men for the glory of God. The Spirit of Christ animated the prophets and indwelt them as those speaking on behalf of God (1 Peter 1:11). Abraham himself, called a prophet, had the Spirit indwelling him (Gen. 20:6). Even Joseph is said to have the Spirit of God in him when Pharaoh commented, "Can we find such a man as this – a man *in whom* the Spirit of God is?" (Gen. 41:38). The blessing of Abraham and the promise of the Spirit were always bestowed upon all those that believed God and His promises.

Are more people converted after the coming of Christ by the Spirit than before the coming of Christ by the Spirit? Why do you think so?

_____
_____
_____
_____

Though the Spirit may have been more sparingly imparted, this never voided the same work of the Spirit in the Old Testament as in the New Testament (Num. 11:17; 27:18; Deut. 34:9; Neh. 9:20; Isa 63:11-14). Even in the book of Judges we find God raising up supernaturally gifted men who were endowed with a special portion of the Spirit for service. The prophets themselves required the operation of the Spirit in order to fulfill their special duties as well as being carried along by the Holy Spirit to write the inspired Scriptures. Even the kings, such as David, were endowed with special office-gifts in order to fulfill their function as king.

Find five verses in the prophets that demonstrate the work of the Spirit in the Old Testament.

_____
_____
_____
_____
_____

There are certainly a host of passages that deal with the work of the Holy Spirit through the Old Testament. Psalm 139:7 says, "Where can I go from Your Spirit? Or where can I flee from Your presence?" Psalm 51:11 states, "Do not cast me away from Your presence, And do not take Your Holy Spirit from me." Psalm 143:10 says, "Teach me to do Your will, For You are my God; Your Spirit is good. Lead me in the land of uprightness." Paul the apostle quotes Psalm 116:10, "And since we have the same spirit of faith, according to what is written, "I believed and therefore I spoke," we also believe and therefore speak," (2 Cor. 4:13). The same Spirit of faith in the Old Testament is the *same* of the New Testament. Even Proverbs 1:23 says, "Turn at my rebuke; Surely I will pour out my spirit on you; I will make my words known to you." Such a pouring out of the Spirit is not uncommon for those seeking truth.

The prophets also have a great amount to say about the Holy Spirit. Hosea 9:7 states that Hosea himself was *a man of the Spirit*. Joel 2:28 prophesies about the restoration of Israel and the outpouring of the Spirit in connection with the Messianic sending of the Spirit. Isaiah sets forth a vivid picture of the Spirit in numerous passages (Isa. 9:2; 42:1; 44:3; 59:19-21; 61:1). Ezekiel was extraordinarily involved in the Spirit's prophetic work (Ezek. 2:24; 8:3; 11:24; 36:25-27). This demonstrates that the Holy Spirit was active in the Old Testament in the work of imparting the superhuman gift of prophecy to a few, and the comforting power of the Spirit to many. The divine personality of the Spirit was not less known and not less recognized in the Old Testament in comparison to the New Testament. Even through the Old Testament the Holy Spirit was recognized as a divine Person.

"The Scripture seems in many places to speak of love in Christians as if it were the same with the Spirit of God in them, or at least as the prime and most natural breathing and acting of the Spirit in the soul," (*Unpublished Essay on the Trinity*).

Jonathan Edwards (1703-1758)

 Read Phil. 2:1.

Edwards believed the natural outworking of the fellowship of believers is love. Love is only possible by the indwelling of the Spirit. What does Edwards mean when he says this is, "as the prime and most natural breathing and acting of the Spirit in the soul?"

_____
_____
_____
_____
_____

In the New Testament the Spirit's work is more clearly seen, but at no time was His work *ever* called into question. Jesus and the apostles in speaking of the Spirit's work were not speaking some new language that threw off their hearers. The fundamental idea that the Messiah should be anointed with the Spirit and come in the power of the Spirit was consistent with what the Jews understood in that day.

The Divinity of the Holy Spirit

All the Gospel evangelists refer to the Spirit's work in connection with His birth, baptism and temptation. But the titles *Christ* or *Messiah* were given to the Redeemer from the peculiar unction of the Spirit which was given to him by nature and degree. In terms of the coming of the Messiah, the forerunner, John the Baptist, was *filled* with the Spirit even from his mother's womb (Luke 1:15-17). Elizabeth, Zacharias, and Simeon were *filled* with the Holy Spirit and gave forth divine announcements of the divine will (Luke 1:42, 67, 2:25). With Christ, though, it is very much different. The infinite fullness of the Spirit was given to Him constantly and uninterruptedly unlike believers who had the Spirit indwelling them, but not uninterruptedly. There was a time when believers did not have the Spirit, and now do. Jesus *always* had the fullness of His Spirit dwelling in Him, even from his conception. His Father's will was to send the Holy Spirit in His name (John 14:26) and that the Spirit would be dispensed by His own hand.

With the teachings of Christ, there are two main divisions about the Spirit, 1) those which describe the Spirit's work in conversion, and 2) those which describe the Spirit's work on the mind of the apostles and of the Church in general. Oftentimes, the teaching of the Spirit surrounded discourses on living water (John 7:37-39). Such blessings are announced as gifts to those that come and repent of their sins. This is done by faith which involves the teaching of the Father (John 6:45), the work of the Son (John 12:32) and the life-giving power of the Spirit (John 6:63).

When the apostle speaks of the Spirit not yet being *given* as with the apostle John, he is not talking about *location*.

If the Spirit is God, and is omnipresent, how can he be "given" by the Father and the Son? Explain.

_____
_____
_____
_____
_____

The Spirit is everywhere, where He will be forever and will never be in any other place since He is infinite. When the Apostles says, "the Spirit was not yet given" (John 7:39) he is speaking *comparatively*, not absolutely, as is always the case between the Old Testament and the New Testament. Nor is it strange when Christ says, "Receive ye the Holy Spirit (John 20:22)." This refers to the gifting of the Holy Spirit for service, in which the apostles would take up in Jerusalem. They would receive even more of the Spirit in Jerusalem as they awaited a greater outpouring for their Gospel service.

The greatest event in all of history next to the incarnation, death and resurrection of Jesus Christ is the giving of the Comforter by the Messiah. The formal Christian economy following the Messiah was inaugurated at Pentecost. Here the Holy Spirit took the place of Christ's physical bodily presence, and instead, was sent to fill that void spiritually. Now the enthroned Messiah seated at the right hand of God would send the Holy Spirit. He would not simply proceed form the Father and the Son, but he would be sent by the Messiah for the specific task of organically uniting the body of which the Messiah is the Head. The Spirit was poured out upon the one hundred and twenty of the upper room – those who waited upon the Lord's command. The tongues of fire baptized them for *service*, and touched them on their heads. This effusion of the Spirit made a great change on all the powers of the apostles, whether we look at the further sanctification of their heart (since they had previously been converted) or their empowerment for service. The extraordinary gifts given to these men by the Holy Spirit would cease after the Church was founded upon the inspired Scripture. Gifts such as tongues (1 Cor. 14:22), the interpretation of tongues (1 Cor. 14:5), the word of wisdom (1 Cor. 12:8), the gift of faith (Mark 16:18; Acts 28:5) – which is not the same as faith in believing, but the faith of miracles – the power of discerning spirits, the gifts of healing, and other gifts which were supernatural of the Holy Spirit, were given to the Apostles, but sovereignly disposed by the Spirit to them in His own right for *founding* the church.

The apostolic Epistles demonstrate an acute awareness of the person and work of the Holy Spirit. Paul draws attention to the reality that Christ and the Spirit work together for the good of the church and the glory of God (2 Cor. 3:17).

Match the Scripture to the designation.
2 Cor. 4:13; 1 Cor. 2:14; Rom. 8:15; 1 Cor. 6:11; Rom. 8:9; Rom. 8:11; Gal. 4:6; Rom 8:11; Heb. 10:29

Spirit of God	_____
Spirit of His Son	_____
Spirit of Him that raised up Christ from the dead	_____
Spirit of Grace	_____
Spirit of Adoption	_____
Spirit that dwells in us	_____
The Spirit washes, sanctifies and justifies His church	_____
The Spirit reveals His word to His people	_____
The Spirit is the author of saving faith	_____

The work, seen here thus far, is the same work that the Spirit accomplishes all through redemptive history, whether in the Old Testament or New Testament. The contrast between one and the other mainly rests on the extent the Spirit was given to the Messiah's rule and reign, and His actions to send the Spirit from the throne of God. In comparison with the numbers of people who had the Spirit in the Old Testament, and were made partakers of the Spirit, Paul makes a differentiation between the economy of the "letter" and the economy of the "Spirit" (2 Cor. 3:6). It is by the scope and extent of the outpouring of the Spirit that marks the difference. The Spirit is given in a great extent (to more people) post-resurrection than pre-resurrection.

In the practical application of the work of the Spirit upon the Christian, one may divide His work into the three sections that Romans outlines: regeneration, spiritual-mindedness, and walking after the Spirit (Romans 8:4, 6, 9). Such a gracious salvation and indwelling of the spirit (walking in Him) is of the Christian in any age. For, Paul says in Romans 8:9, "But you are not in the flesh but in the Spirit, if indeed the Spirit of God dwells in you. Now if anyone does not have the Spirit of Christ, he is not His." If one does not "have" the Spirit, meaning to have, *i.e.* to hold in the sense of wearing, then He is not God's and not Christ's. He addresses those who walk after the Spirit, of whom we have to understand contrary things to the former. He defines what it is to be in the Spirit, or to be sanctified, that is, to have the Spirit of God dwelling in us. Then he declares that sanctification is so joined and knit to our grafting into Christ, that it can by no means be separated. However, he says that anyone who does not have the Spirit in this way is not of Christ, or not saved. Upon this verse alone, it is eminently apparent that all the saints, in any sage, were saved, filled, and walking in the Spirit in this sense or they were not of Christ in any saving sense. On this ground they are evidenced to be children of the Spirit, adopted by God, and having a filial relationship with God as His children.

[
"Every heart that is not a Holy Spirit Temple is nothing more than Satan's hideous dunghill," (*The Marks of a Godly Man*).
Daniel Burgess (1645-1713)
]

For the Christian, the Spirit is also the Spirit of prayer (Eph. 1:17; James 1:26) and by the illumination of the Spirit, the Christian is able to understand the things of God and of Christ which helps the believer to pray effectively according to the will of God. The Spirit is also the Christian's seal and earnest (Eph. 1:13; 4:30). This means that believers are God's inviolable property and known to be so by the Spirit dwelling in them.

One of the most comprehensive treatments of the New Testament witness to the Spirit is through the Apostle John and his letters. The Spirit is known as the Spirit of God (1 John 4:2), sent forth from God (1 John 4:3), providing powerful unction from the Holy One (1 John 2:20-27), the Spirit of truth (1 John 5:6), and the One who abides in us (1 John 3:24).

In speaking of the divine procession of the Spirit, there are two ways of looking at this subject: 1) *a priori*, (relating to or denoting reasoning or knowledge that proceeds from theoretical deduction rather than from observation or experience), from the fact of eternal procession, and 2) *a posteriori*, (relating to or denoting reasoning or knowledge that proceeds from observations or experiences to the deduction of probable causes.), from the unquestionable evidences of divine personality which are given all through the Scriptures. The divine personality is proven against the Arian and Sabellian heresies which have attempted to overthrow this doctrine in the church through the ages. Sabellius believed that the Holy Spirit was merely a divine *influence* that was part of the three masks of God. Arius believed that the Spirit was simply a created force used *by* God. Both are *heretically* (*damningly*) wrong. When the Bible speaks about the personality of the Spirit, it speaks in terms of mind, will, and spontaneous action. It is important to note that the term "person" is not a biblical term and is very much capable of being twisted and turned to suit a heretical notion. It is most helpful, then, to define the Spirit and arrive at the definition than to define "person" and suit the Scriptures to a man-made definition. In creating a definition, it would be most helpful to give the Spirit descriptive character traits based on Scripture first. In this way we can extract a definition instead of creating one to overlay what men believe "person" should mean.

The Spirit is not the Father and is not the Son, but distinct from both. He is intelligent, has a will, power, and wisdom that He acts upon. Jesus said He would send another Comforter, which, if Christ is the first Comforter, than that statement alone demonstrates the personality of *mind, will, and affections of another Comforter*. If the Spirit is denied as a person from that text (John 14:16-17), "And I will pray the Father, and He will give you another Helper, that He may abide with you forever "the Spirit of truth," then one must also deny the personality of the Christ, which is impossible.

The Spirit teaches (John 14:26), guides (John 16:13), and glorifies Christ (John 16:14). The change of gender in John 16 to the demonstrative pronoun (*eikenos*) demonstrates personality when it refers to "He" all through the passage referring to the Spirit. The personality of the Spirit, then, may be placed under the following six categories: 1) The personal actions ascribed to Him abundantly prove his personality (John 14:26; 1 Cor. 12:11). 2) His distinction from the Father and the Son, and His mission from both, prove His personality (John 15:26). 3) The co-ordinate rank and power that belong to Him equally with the Father and the Son prove His personality (Matt. 28:19; 2 Cor. 13:14). 4) His appearance under a visible form at the baptism of Christ and on the day of Pentecost proves His personality. 5) The sin against the Holy Ghost implying a Person proves His personality. 6) The way in which He is distinguished from His gifts proves His personality (1 Cor. 12:11).

["The property of the Holy Spirit is to be breathed, to be sent forth and to proceed from the Father and the Son. John 15:26, "He whom I will send forth you from the Father, that Spirit of truth who proceeds from the Father: Romans 8:9, "the Spirit of Christ," Galatians 4:6, "the Spirit of the Son," (*Marrow of Theology*).
William Ames (1576-1645)]

What does William Ames mean when he says "the *property* of the Holy Spirit is to be breathed?"

_____
_____
_____
_____
_____

In terms of the procession of the Spirit, He proceeds from the Father and the Son. John 15:26 says, "whom I shall send to you from the Father, the Spirit of truth who proceeds from the Father, He will testify of Me." The term "proceeds" signifies an ever-enduring procession. The Spirit proceeds forever from the Father. He also proceeds from the Son. John 16:14 states, "He will glorify Me, for He will take of what is Mine and declare it to you." The Son is eternally generated from the Father, and hears what the Father commands and speaks. The Spirit proceeds from them both in order to speak what He hears the Son teach. As John 16:13 says, "for He will not speak on His own authority, but whatever He hears He will speak; and

He will tell you things to come."

Read each of the verses in parenthesis. In terms of the deity of the Spirit, it is proved by the procession of the Spirit from God, and the incommunicable acts of creation and providence as ascribed to the Spirit (Gen. 1:6; Psalm 33:6; Job 26:13). Divine attributes are ascribed to Him (1 Cor. 2:10-11; Psalm 139:7; Romans 8:26; 1 Cor. 1:13). He is placed in rank with the Father and the Son (such as at Christ's baptism – Matthew 3:16), and the name of God is directly given to Him (Acts 5:3-4; cf. Psalm 95:7 and Heb. 3:7).

The work of the Spirit in the anointing of Christ, according to His work in the Covenant of Grace, is of great importance. The Lord Jesus taught about the nature of the Covenant when He spoke of Himself as receiving the Father's command (John 10:18), and of the Spirit as not speaking of Himself, but glorifying Christ, and of taking of His teachings and showing them to the disciples (John 16:14).

The great fact of the incarnation of the Son in human flesh takes for granted that Christ's manhood was immediately filled and led by the Spirit. Passages that refer to Christ being filled with the Spirit, or the Spirit given to Him without measure, are stated historically, not theologically. They are part of the historical *narrative* of the Gospels. In the office of Mediator, in human flesh, the Lord Jesus received the unction of the Spirit. As the humanity was assumed in the hypostatic union (the union between the flesh and the divinity of the Son of God) the person of Christ was anointed by the Spirit so far as the call to the office was concerned. At the same time, his humanity is anointed as far as the actual supplies of gifts and graces are concerned, so that He has a necessary endowment for the function of His office.

The first degree of this anointing of the Spirit took place at his incarnation (Luke 1:35; Luke 2:40). The second degree was given at His baptism (John 1:33). This descent was intended to confirm and encourage the Lord Jesus before entering on his formal work of salvation. The symbolic dove demonstrated the resting of the Spirit upon Him for the task (Isaiah 11:2). The

Spirit anointed Him supremely for His official work (Matthew 3:11). This was also part of His temptation in the wilderness where the Spirit drove Him there to be tested. And when such a time of testing was completed, Luke tells us that He returned with the power of the Spirit (Luke 4:14). When He offered Himself upon the cross as an oblation (sacrifice), He did this through the power of the Spirit. Hebrews 9:14 states, "how much more shall the blood of Christ, who through the eternal Spirit offered Himself without spot to God, cleanse your conscience from dead works to serve the living God?" The Son of God, moved and animated by the Holy Spirit, offered Himself without spot or blemish as an atoning sacrifice.

The third degree of Christ's unction is for His exaltation. Acts 2:33 says, "Therefore being exalted to the right hand of God, and having received from the Father the promise of the Holy Spirit, He poured out this which you now see and hear." This is where the actual *mission* of the Comforter is stated and is sent by the Messiah from His throne room to the Church organically binding together the whole Church to the Head. In the Old Testament the Holy Spirit is never actually said to be "sent" since this would be done officially by the office of the *Mediator*.

 Read John 3:1-10.

When Jesus says, "Art thou a master of Israel, and knowest not these things?" what is he saying about the teaching of the Holy Spirit? Why should Nicodemas have known about regeneration? Is this a new idea or old idea?

_____
_____
_____
_____

Should Christians believe the Scriptures are inspired and a production of the Holy Spirit? Extraordinary gifts were given to the church through the Old and New Testaments for service. The Spirit is given authorship of these gifts (Hebrews 2:4). Such is the case with the Holy Spirit carrying along the prophets to speak and write down the Word of God. Peter states, "for prophecy never came by the will of man, but holy men of God spoke as they were moved by the Holy Spirit (2 Peter 1:21)." The prophetic Spirit imparted a supernatural divine illumination in virtue of what the apostles and prophets understood fully and what they were commissioned to announce on behalf of God and Christ. This would include miracles that immediately prove the truth of the doctrine and the inspiration of the messenger. The Holy Spirit accommodated the message through prophets which resembles a mother's accommodation to the capacity of her infant. He spoke in a manner that human beings would understand the divine message.

Spiritual illumination of the believer is different than being carried along by the Spirit to confer a divine message. Conferring divine revelation was officially binding upon the church, where divine illumination helps the believer understand the Word of God.

The Spirit applies the work of redemption to the individual in what theology calls *regeneration*. The efficacious operation of the Spirit presupposes God's sovereign election on certain individuals to receive the benefits of Christ's death for them. This application of Christ's work is done by the Spirit's divine application on the human soul, or heart.

Since Adam forfeited the Spirit in the garden, it is now part of the history of redemption to gain back the Spirit by God's gracious work through Christ and through the Spirit's work on the heart. Men do not have the Spirit as fallen humans (Jude 19), and as a necessary consequence of that void, they are sensual and carnal (1 Cor. 2:14). This withdrawal of the Spirit is called "spiritual death," (2 Cor. 3:5; 1 Cor. 2:14; Romans 8:7). Now, men must be regenerated and endowed with the Spirit of God since they are imputed with Adam's sin from conception and are devoid of all spiritual good.

> "Generation lost us, it must be regeneration that recovers us," (*The Doctrine of Regeneration and the New Birth*).
> Isaac Ambrose (1604-1664)

What does Ambrose mean when he says "generation?"

_____
_____
_____
_____
_____

Jesus demonstrates, emphatically, that men must be born again, or born from above, which is the work of regeneration on the heart of the wicked (John 3:3). As John 6:63 states, "It is the Spirit who gives life; the flesh profits nothing." Such a sovereign regeneration (a change of the heart from stone to beating flesh) is by the blowing will of the Spirit (John 3:1-8). The Spirit then convicts and sanctifies the individual by purging unbelief (John 16:8). Those that are regenerated are then made new creatures (2 Cor. 5:17). The Spirit inhabits the whole man and renews him (Romans 8:9). These are adopted as sons, and are assured by the Spirit of their sovereign election (Rom. 8:16; 1 John 3:2).

Did the Spirit inhabit and renew Abraham? Why or why not?

_____
_____
_____
_____

In the work of sanctification it is important to note the work of Christ for the Christian in comparison to the work of the Spirit in the Christian. One leads to a first conversion, the other to a continual holiness.

The Spirit enables regenerated Christians to discern good from evil, or sin from holiness. He disposes the mind to accept truth and to know what the Scriptures contain. Here the Spirit aids the Christian in expounding Scripture in order to apply that Scripture to the Christian's life and further grow in the mystical union he now has with Christ (1 Cor. 6:17). The Spirit illuminates through His indwelling presence within the individual (John 16:16; 2 Tim. 1:14; Rom. 8:9; Gal. 4:6; 1 Cor. 3:16; 1 John 4:13; Eph. 1:13).

Those who are illuminated and are indwelt by the Spirit are called by the Spirit (Gal 5:18; Rom. 8:14; Ezek. 36:27). The grand security for the perseverance of the saints is the leading of the Spirit. However, the Baptism of the Spirit is given for leading and service in a far wider manner in comparison to the Old Testament. In the New Testament His function is poured out over the whole covenant community, and in the Old Testament He chose specific people to be more or less anointed for service.

The new Spirit-led ethical actions of the Christian come after regeneration and the indwelling of the Spirit. Christian ethics are an immediate result of the Spirit's work on the believer. They are never isolated from Christ or the relations of His kingdom and are communicated to Christians by the Spirit through the Word. Love is the principle here, and only through the power of the Spirit can there be true Christian love reflecting Christ (1 Cor. 13).

The degree of the Christian's sanctification and ethics will differ according to the Spirit's will. Romans 7 describes for us a glimpse into the real struggle in which every believer fights against sin. They sometimes lose and sometimes win. Ultimately they will be glorified. But the Spirit of grace enables them to fight their way out of every temptation, (1 Cor. 10:13) although believers do not always arrest that opportunity to please God and rather, they grieve the Spirit. As Ephesians 4:30 says, "And do not grieve the Holy Spirit of God, by whom you were sealed for the day of redemption."

As a Christian, indwelt by the Spirit of God, what would be left spiritually in you if the Spirit of God could be "removed" from you?

_____
_____
_____
_____
_____

Besides the indwelling of the Spirit of God in you, what other *good*, aside from the Spirit's work in you, *is in you*? In other words, what good in you do *you* contribute in you?

_____
_____
_____
_____
_____

The Church is the organic completion of the united body to the Head – Jesus Christ. Christ's cause on the earth is advanced through the Spirit, through individuals who are indwelt by the Spirit. The Holy Spirit joins together every regenerated member of the Church to the Head to create a complete body. The Church of Christ always had office bearers, and was never without office bearers though in different ages these offices differed in respect to their outward administrations. The Church has a twofold function: 1) a holy society in the world maintaining a separation from the world for worship, and 2) a missionary institute with a view to propagate or extend the Gospel to them that are without (1 Peter 2:5; John 15:1-6). There is and has only been one church and one Spirit in the Old Testament and the New Testament. The same Spirit of faith in the New Testament filled believers in the Old Testament (2 Cor. 4:13).

At various points through the history of the church, the Spirit has more or less been seen in operation. For example, there are three main epochs in which the miraculous giftedness of the Spirit worked through the church for the good of the church: 1) in the days of Moses, 2)

The Divinity of the Holy Spirit

in the days of Elijah, and 2) in the days of the Messiah and his apostles. At other times, such as the Great Awakenings under the preaching of men like Jonathan Edwards, we find curious outpourings of the Spirit on His people for the purpose of revival and sanctification. In all cases, the mission of the church (to convert souls and proclaim the kingdom) and the primary relationship of the church to Christ (to worship God) have never changed.

{ "In the very earliest literature, in the apostolic Fathers, and in the Epistle of Clemens especially, there are a host of allusions to the Holy Spirit. The circular letter issued by the church of Smyrna after Polycarp's death is of the same nature. The church has never been afraid to say in its corpus of writings and literature about theological issues, "I believe in the Holy Spirit," (*Systematic Theology*).
Charles Hodge (1797-1878) }

The Decrees of God

"When he made a decree for the rain, and a way for the lightning of the thunder: Then did he see it, and declare it; he prepared it, yea, and searched it out. And unto man he said, Behold, the fear of the Lord, that is wisdom; and to depart from evil is understanding," (Job. 28:26-28).

The decrees of God (God's judicial decisions) are His eternal purpose, according to the counsel of His will, whereby for His own glory He hath foreordained whatsoever comes to pass. Here we see the end or final cause contemplated in all God's decrees which is their accomplishment for His own glory. All His decrees are all reducible to *one eternal purpose*. They are free and sovereign, determined by the counsel of His own will; and, they comprehend all events.

What is the one reason why God decrees *anything*? Use Scripture to prove it.

_____
_____
_____
_____
_____

["God works nothing but what he first decreed, and he brings all his decrees to pass by his works," (*The Vision of the Wheels*).

Matthew Mead (1629-1699)]

The final cause of *all* God's purposes *is His own glory*. Revelation 4:11 states, "Thou art worthy, O Lord, to receive glory, and honor, and power: for thou hast created all things, and for thy pleasure they are and were created." All things are said to be not only of God and through Him, but *for Him*. God frequently announces His determination to make *His glory* known. "As truly as I live, all the earth shall be filled with the glory of the Lord," (Num. 14:21). "For mine own sake, even for mine own sake, will I do it; for how should my name be polluted? and I will not give my glory unto another," (Isa. 48:11). "I wrought for my name's sake, that it should not be polluted before the heathen," (Ezek. 20:9). Even though men are saved from sin, they are saved for God's glory, and redemption is designed to reveal the glory of God (1 Cor. 1:26-31; Eph. 2:8-10). It is characteristic of the Bible that it places God first, and the good of the creation second. The glory of God is the end of all His decrees. The decrees of God, therefore, are not many, but one purpose. They are all parts of one all-comprehending plan. God never purposes what He did not originally intend; or that one part of his plan is independent of other parts. It is one scheme, and therefore one purpose.

The Decrees of God are *eternal* as God is eternal. This follows from the perfection of His divine Being. He sees the end from the beginning and all of time stands before Him as an instantaneous moment. Distinctions of time have no reference to Him who inhabits *eternity*. The salvation of men is said to be, "according to the eternal purpose which He purposed in Christ Jesus," (Eph. 3:11). Believers were chosen in Christ, "before the foundation of the world," (Eph. 1:4). Christ as a sacrifice was, "foreordained before the foundation of the world, but was manifest in these last times for you, who by Him do believe in God," (1 Pet. 1:20-21, cf. Rom. 9:33-36 and Acts 2:23).

The decrees of God are also immutable. To God the causes of change have no existence. With God there is, "no variableness, neither shadow of turning," (James 1:17). And we hear the Psalmist say, "The counsel of the Lord standeth forever, the thoughts of his heart to all generations," (Psa. 33:11). Isaiah writes, "The Lord of hosts hath sworn, saying, Surely as I have thought, so shall it come to pass; and as I have purposed, so shall it stand," (Isa. 14:24). The Scriptures teach that He, "doeth whatsoever He pleaseth," (Psa. 115:3).

The decrees of God are efficacious (always effectual). They render *certain* the end to what He decrees. Whatever God ordains will come to pass. God has a plan. If that plan includes all events, to bring it to pass, then all events stand in mutual relation and dependence to His purpose. There could be no certainty of an outcome to glorify God if the decrees of God were not efficacious. There would be no assurance of any event, or even of a prophecy. All ground of confidence in God would be lost without such efficacy.

Does anything ever happen that God is surprised about? Why or why not?
___
___
___
___
___

If God's plan is efficacious, then every event is foreordained by God as *certain* to come to pass. As the *Westminster Confession* states, God ordains, "whatsoever comes to pass." God works all things according to the counsel of His will. All things are, in fact, *all things*. The Bible teaches that God decrees the free acts of men, divine prophecy, sinful acts, as well as holy acts. Acts 2:23 states, for example, "Him, being delivered by the determinate counsel and foreknowledge of God, ye have taken, and by wicked hands have crucified and slain." Acts 4:27 also states, "For of a truth against thy holy child Jesus, whom thou hast anointed, both Herod and Pontius Pilate, with the Gentiles and the people of Israel were gathered together, for to do whatsoever thy hand and thy counsel determined before to be done." The cross, a sinful act whereby men killed the Son of God, was ordained by God to take place. It was the greatest crime ever committed. It is therefore beyond all doubt Biblically sound to teach and believe that sin is foreordained by God.

When God makes it rain, and the grass gets wet, what makes the grass wet?
___
___
___

Secondary causes (like the rain making the grass wet) are not abolished by God's decree, but rather, are established. Man's will, the wetness of the grass, a sinkhole that collapses a road, autism in children, or a host of other effects based on some previous cause are not abolished because God decrees a specific end. God ordains the *means* as well as the end to the glorification of Himself.

THE ETERNAL COUNSEL OF GOD AND HIS WILL

When we investigate the core of the eternal counsel of God, we find the cross staring back. When looking intensely at the cross, we see the Continuum. The Continuum is the outlaid plan of God's decrees set down in his mind in order of that which will come to pass. All this is wrapped up within a neat package that Orthodox Christianity has labeled "God's Eternal Counsel." When mentioning the counsel of God I do not mean to say that God consults other beings which may surround Him—as lawyers consult a judge or the president of a corporation confides in His board of trustees. What I mean is that God confides *in* Himself. God centers the entirety of the eternal counsel upon His own idea. Whenever we look at Scripture there is a repeated indication that God is doing something around a purpose or an intended end; God has an intention in everything He does. And what lies in the pages of Scripture are those things which God uses to accomplish His end. They may be people, events, armies, nations, or those things He finds useful in His own discretion. Unfortunately, some deny the existence of any such Counsel and therefore derange the very essence of God Himself. For, if He has no purpose, then our understanding of His attributes becomes estranged in obscurity, and God becomes irrational.

Read the following Scriptures which speak *clearly* of God's eternal counsel: Judges 18:5, 20:18; 1 Samuel 14:37; Ezra 10:3; Psalm 16:7, 33:11, 73:24, 106:13, 107:11; Proverbs 19:21; Isaiah 5:19, 25:1, 28:29, 46:10-11; Jeremiah 23:18, 22, 32:19, 49:20, 50:45; Micah 4:12; Luke 7:30; Acts 2:23, 20:27; Ephesians 1:11; Hebrews 6:17; Revelation 3:18.

> "The counsel of God is, as it were, his deliberation over the best manner of accomplishing anything already approved by the understanding and the will," (*Marrow of Theology*).
> William Ames (1576-1645)

Is there any possibility that God's plan could change somewhere along the timeline? Why or why not?

_____
_____
_____
_____
_____

The counsel of God cannot change, and there is no better plan to execute or to improve on. The eternal counsel of God has been, is, and will be just as it has always been since it rests in the nature of God. Those who would create a counsel which is mutable would immediately destroy, so to speak, the eternal counsel of God *theologically*.

ALL THINGS COME FROM GOD'S COUNSEL

We can see from Scripture that all things come from God and these things are part of His intended plan. Paul writes in Colossians 1:16-17, "By Him all things consist." We read in Genesis chapter 1, "In the beginning God created the heavens and the earth." Everything which exists had its origin in God. Light and darkness, oceans and seas, the sky and space, animals, birds, fish, and human beings all come from the handiwork of God according to Genesis 1:31; and everything He made was very good. In this complete plan God providentially tends to all areas in which He deals with His creation.

Challenge

Read all the verses proving this paragraph in parenthesis. You can find this paragraph outlined in Loraine Boettner's book, *"The Reformed Doctrine of Predestination."*

> God's plan is eternal and executes all things from that plan over creation (2 Timothy 1:9; Psalm 33:11; Isaiah 37:26, 46:9; 2 Thessalonians 2:13; Matthew 25:34; 1 Peter 1:20; Jeremiah 31:3; Acts 15:18; Psalm 139:16). God's plan is unchangeable in regards to His intentions for created beings (James 1:17; Isaiah 14:24, 46:10; Numbers 23:19; Malachi 3:6). The divine plan of God includes the future acts of men (Daniel 2:28; John 6:64; Matthew 20:18-19) and prophecies, which are predictions of future events (Micah 5:2; Matthew 2:5-6, 27:9; Luke 2:1-7; Psalm 22:18; John 19:24, 29, 33, 36, 37; Psalm 34:19; Zechariah 12:10). The divine plan includes what men would consider "chance" happenings (Proverbs 16:33; Jonah 1:7; Acts 1:24, 26; Job 5:6, 36:32; 1 Kings 22:28; Mark 14:30; Genesis 37:28, 45:5; 1 Samuel 9:5-10, 15, 16). Some events are recorded as fixed or certain, like prophecies and oracles (Luke 21:24, 22:22; John 8:20; Matthew 24:26; Genesis 41:32; Habakkuk 2:3; Jeremiah 15:2, 27:7; Job 14:15). Even the sinful acts of men are included in the plan and are overruled for good (Genesis 50:20; Isaiah 45:7; Amos 3:6; Acts 3:18; Matthew 21:42; Romans 8:28).

The most important aspect of His creation was the pinnacle of all He had done, namely, human beings created in His image. These human beings were a direct result of the eternal counsel, "Then God said, 'Let us make man in our image, in our likeness, and let them rule over [the inhabitants of the earth].'" The consultation within the divine Godhead was an act of His eternal counsel and plan. It was the actuation of the Continuum within the sphere of time. It was the physical manifestation of Adam and Eve within the "sphere" of creation.

God's Counsel is actual for God in a different sense than it is actual with us because, as said earlier, we live, move, and exist within space and time, and we must distinguish between the importance of *what* we experience and *how* God experiences. God's counsel in His eternal mind is present at an instant. For us it is an unfolding of a redemptive act seen through the eons of time. We can see the counsel of God acting upon time elsewhere in Scripture, "But the plans of the Lord stand firm forever, the purposes of His heart through all generations (Psalm 33:11)." Through all of time and through countless generations of covenant people the counsel of God's electing love exists. They turn to Him, for they know He is their Creator and all things belong to Him including His people (1 Corinthians 6:19), power (Psalm 62:11), salvation (Psalm 3:8), vengeance (Hebrews 10:30), and secret things which have not been manifested to us (Deuteronomy 29:29). There is an Eternal Counsel by which all things have been brought forth. From within the mind of God, He has brought all things into actuality for His people to enjoy Him.

THE ETERNAL COUNSEL HAS ITS BASE IN GOD'S KNOWLEDGE

Remember that we often speak of God in positive terms, as in being omniscient or "all knowing", or we speak in negative terms, that He is infinite or rather "not finite?" Whenever we speak of the knowledge of God, we must first understand that this knowledge is beyond measure. First, God's knowledge can be seen as all encompassing. It involves every aspect of everything which can be known about anything everywhere. John 21:17 states, "Lord, you know all things." Thus, we can then apply the term, infinite, that God's knowledge is infinite in every way; it is not limited by anything. Unfortunately, when we use terms such as these we are not speaking with any specific words but only in generalities. We can only study what we have, namely Scripture. And Scripture does not go into great detail but gives us many aspects in general terms about God. Yet, Scripture is a *lisp* to us. It is baby talk from an infinite God to finite humans. This is what we call the doctrine of God's incomprehensibility, and Calvin called it the *doctrine of accommodation*. The finite cannot contain the infinite. God is so transcendent and exalted that our finite, depraved minds could not possibly contain a *minutia* of what God knows, much less all of it.

The Decrees of God

["God knows all things perfectly, undividedly, distinctly, and immutably," (*Institutes of Elenctic Theology*, Volume 1).
Francis Turretin (1623-1687)]

Explain how Scripture is a lisp to us as humans, and that the Bible is finite though God is infinite.

_____
_____
_____
_____
_____

God knows things perfectly because He knows all things *by himself*. Since He is perfect as to His divine essence, all things which He knows are known perfectly. Berkhof, in his *Systematic Theology*, defines the knowledge of God as, "that perfection of God whereby He, in an entirely unique manner, knows Himself and all things possible and actual in one eternal and most simple act." William Ames, in his Marrow of Theology, speaks of God knowing, "all things by genesis and does not require knowledge through analysis of things; therefore all things are in his mind before they are in themselves."

Is there anything that God does not know? Why or why not?

_____
_____
_____
_____
_____

Read the following Scriptures that attest to the fact that God knows all things (John 21:17; 1 John 3:20; Acts 15:18; Hebrews 4:13; Psalm 94:11, 103:14, 139:1-4; Jeremiah 1:5; Matthew 10:30; 1 Corinthians 2:7; Romans 8:29; Ephesians 1:4; John 8:26; Job 37:16; 1 Samuel 2:3; Psalm 94:9; Isaiah 29:15). God knows the inclinations of a man's heart (1 Samuel 16:7); He knows men's ways (Job 23:10); He knows about things both good and evil (Proverbs 15:3) and all things which enter into the mind of every man (Ezekiel 11:15). God's knowledge is seen in the term "light" (1 John 1:5; 1 Timothy 6:16; Psalm 4:7, 27:1, 36:10, 43:3; John 1:4, 9, 8:12; James 1:17). When we see God as "light," we mean that He is designated as perfect in self-consciousness and thus sees all things contingent to Him perfectly. "Light" shows God as having no darkness in Him and being completely pure and holy.

GOD'S FOREKNOWLEDGE AND THE ETERNAL COUNSEL

How do we know that God does *not* look down the corridor of time to see what happens and then chooses to do things based on what he sees?

_____
_____
_____
_____
_____

God does not foresee something and base His eternal decree on a contingent factor. His eternal decree creates contingent beings, but it is not based on contingent beings or actions at all. God has freely ordained some to eternal life and some to eternal death as a result of God's good pleasure.

> "The good pleasure of God is an act of the divine will freely and effectively determining all things...As for intention, there is no foreknowledge which is prerequisite or presupposed for the decree of predestination besides that simple intelligence which relates to all things, since it depends upon no cause, reason, or outward condition, but proceeds purely from the will of him who predestines," (*Marrow of Theology*).
>
> William Ames (1576-1645)

Ames says that predestination does not depend on anything but God's will. How does that make you feel concerning your salvation, and the possible "non-salvation" of a relative you might be praying for?

_____
_____
_____
_____
_____

As the *Westminster Confession* states, "God, from all eternity, did, by the most wise and holy counsel of His own will, freely and unchangeably ordain whatsoever comes to pass." God is actual. Everything which resides within the mind of God is not potential but is an eternal actual. A fancy name given to this actuality, so finite human beings can grasp the idea in some sense, is the *eternal decree*. The eternal decree of God is that perfect, complete, infinite plan from which all things transpire in time and space as history unfolds. It is the will of God on any specific act or intention derived from His omniscience concerning any given thing. It is the next step in understanding the eternal counsel; or more appropriately, what God *did* in that counsel.

What are some of the most "mundane" and "basic" things that God has eternally decreed? Name 5 in your own life. For example, the amount of lint (in grams) in your dryer basket next Tuesday.

_____

_____

_____

_____

_____

God has planned this decree carefully and to its most minute detail. Jesus says, "Are not two sparrows sold for a penny? Yet not one of them will fall to the ground apart from the will of your Father. And even the very hairs on your head are all numbered" (Matthew 10:29, 30). How infinite is this where God Himself numbers the hairs on your head! He is there when every sparrow falls, for His plan is that vast. He leaves nothing to chance nor anything to a whimsical fling. All things are under His power and authority, and all things have been planned accordingly, (Genesis 50:20; Psalm 75:9-25; John 10:29).

The decrees of God are purpose-filled. It is the will of God *willing*. It is the very essence of His actions seen in the Continuum, redeeming man from His awful state. It is the incarnation, death, and resurrection which is at the heart of this great decree. God's knowledge is no doubt eternal, as is His essence. Therefore, it is necessary that the decree upon which it is set forth is also eternal. Every decree of God is eternal. We lower God's standards when we see that God's redemptive, eternal plan rests on the will of man. For, if God is so impotent that He must wait on man for His will to be effectual, then He is hardly a God at all. All things are decreed by God in an eternal and unchangeable covenant. This decree takes place at an appointed time and nothing can change it, for if it could change then the Continuum would fall and cease to be eternally immutable. This would contradict the Scriptures (Isaiah 46:10; Ephesians 1:9; Matthew 18:7, 26:54; Luke 22:22; Acts 2:23; 1 Corinthians 11:19). Even the most casual of instances are seen as part of the divine decree: accidental death (Exodus 21:12); casting lots (Proverbs 16:33); the preservation of the bones of Christ (John 19:36).

 Read Proverbs 19:21.

Write down a time when God's plans and your plans were synonymous. Write down a time when they were not – you wanted one thing and God ordained another, and you saw it clearly after the fact.

_____
_____
_____
_____
_____

Some feel that this idea of a "decreed end" removes all hopes of man having a will of his own. They think this would seem to remove "free" will because we would all be reduced to mere puppets. But this is not the case, for the Scriptures tell us that we are indeed *free to do what our will desires*. When we are depraved, we desire depravity (Romans 3, 7:5, 8:12). When we are quickened, we desire the things of God (Romans 5:3; 1 Corinthians 12:31; 1 Thessalonians 5:5). We are truly free, for Scripture would be lying to us if we were not, but we do not have a free will. Our will is always in bondage to what we desire. We are responsible for our actions and conditions which God sets before us. But our actions always arise from our inclinations, and our inclinations can please God or displease Him.

It is not my intention to begin a teaching here on election, reprobation and the like. Keep in mind we are simply dealing with God, his nature and his actions. Suffice it for now to stay in that realm and rest on the nature of God knowing he alone is the all Supreme Ruler and Sovereign King of the Universe.

Concluding Remarks

What have we accomplished in this workbook on the doctrine of God? It would be absurd to say that we have "fabricated" a doctrine here, or created something new. Instead, we have relied on much biblical evidence, church history, and the best theologians of the past 2000 years on this doctrine. We have, though, merely scratched the surface. Generally, systematic theology books are five hundred to two thousand pages. The workbook is but a mere introduction to the doctrine of God, to aid you to delve into a deeper relationship with Christ, and seek out some of the best theological works. Might I suggest a few? Keep in mind, this is "just a few." For experienced Christians, read Calvin's, *Institutes of the Christian Religion*, and then Francis Turretin's, *Institutes of Elenctic Theology*. For the seminary student, or the "arm chair theologian," read Berkhof's, *Systematic Theology*, Bavink's *Reformed Dogmatics* (a few volumes), or WGT Shedd's *Dogmatic Theology*. You can also consider Charles Hodge's *Systematic Theology* in 3 volumes, and RL Dabney's *Systematic Theology*. For the novice Christian, read my work, *Systematic Theology Made Easy*, or Louis Berkhof's *Introduction to Systematic Theology*. There are a host of other works to consider that dive into just the doctrine of God, like Bavink's, *The Doctrine of God*. All of these would be a help to expanding your systematic theology knowledge and bringing you into a deeper relationship with Christ.

One of the best exercises you could do after working through this workbook, and then taking the test at the end, is to absorb the information and main ideas in such a way to be able to replicate them or regurgitate them without the workbook in hand.

Do you think you could explain the doctrine of God, at least in part, to a ten year old? What main points would you consider and what Scriptures would you use?

_____

_____

Concluding Remarks

_____
_____
_____

How has this workbook helped you appreciate *the doctrine of God*?
_____
_____
_____
_____
_____

Various explanations have been given in an attempt to understand what God means when he is communicating anything in human terms or in human actions (anthropomorphisms and anthropopathisms) which we dealt with in workbook 2. This intensifies when thinking through the incarnate God in the man Jesus Christ, or the doctrine of God the Father, or how the Holy Spirit works in the lives of both Old Testament and New Testament saints. We are not dealing with bare theological assertions surrounding the Doctrine of God and His attributes. We further deal with the incarnation of God, where God, in some fantastic fashion, assumed the nature of a human being, and came to save his people.

The Christian should then see the truth behind such statements as, "Be imitators of God (Ephesians 5:1)." As Christians imitate Christ they are imitating God. They really are imitating the interpreted divine mind in the man Jesus Christ. This alone should cause Christian amazement in reflecting God's glory as dear sons and daughters.

Explaining such a theological topic is difficult and this workbook is far from covering such a doctrine of God's nature exhaustively. However, if Christians were to gather just a little from this work, they would begin to see the mind-boggling implications that peer around every theological corner on this issue. If you want to understand the doctrine of God more clearly, then look at *Jesus*. Real expressions of God's mind are seen through the filter of the human nature of Jesus Christ. This holds huge implications on the New Testament alone and all the passages studied in "red." We should take very special notice of them. May we read Scripture in a deeper and more meaningful light knowing that the expression of Christ is truly the expression of the person of the eternal Son of God, and it was the Father who sent the Son to come and die, be raised again, and ascend to the Father in order to send the Spirit for our sanctification. In my mind, the doctrine of God is one of the most relevant and important doctrines we could ever need, or desire. It would now do us well to take even more time to read many of the quoted authors of this workbook in order to understand in even greater detail the nature and work of the God we serve. "Even every one that is called by my name: for I have created him for my glory, I have formed him; yea, I have made him," (Isa. 43:7).

Test Yourself

Take as much time as you need in first studying through your answers and the information contained in the workbook. Then, without going back, answer these questions:

How has this workbook helped you appreciate *the doctrine of God*?

___

Where do we find the doctrine of God outlined?

___

What is systematic theology?

___

How would you define "theology?"

___

What is innate knowledge?

What is the Law of God?

What is Theism?

Name two of the 5 arguments for the existence of God.

Test Yourself

Why is God inconceivable?

_____
_____
_____
_____
_____

Why is God incomprehensible?

_____
_____
_____
_____
_____
_____

How do we know God?

_____
_____
_____
_____
_____

Does God have a nose even though Scripture says he does in Exodus 15:8?

_____
_____
_____
_____
_____

Why does God use human terms to communicate to us?

_____

Define "God."

Define "infinite."

Define "immensity."

Define "eternity."

Define "immutable."

How does the idea of the "movie clip" illustration help you understand God's nature in time?

Define "aseity."

What does it mean that God is simple?

What are the formal terms for "all-knowing and everywhere present?"

Why is God in hell?

How would you define the will of God?

What is the difference between the decretive will and the perceptive will of God?

Define "holiness."

What is the "justice of God?"

How is God good?

Define the sovereignty of God.

Define "trinity."

What is Sabellianism?

What is the hypostatic union?

Explain the economy of the Father, Son and Spirit.

Give three verses and their meaning that Jesus is God.

Give three verses and their meaning that the Spirit is a person.

How man natures does the Son of God, Jesus, have?

How many natures does the Father have?

How many natures does the Spirit have?

Define "merit."

What is regeneration?

What is the decree of God?

The eternal counsel has its basis in what?

In what ways did this workbook bring you closer to Christ?

www.ingramcontent.com/pod-product-compliance
Lightning Source LLC
Chambersburg PA
CBHW080549170426
43195CB00016B/2724